GOODBYE
CHRISTOPHER ROBIN

ALSO BY ANN THWAITE

GOODBYE CHRISTOPHER ROBIN: A. A. MILNE AND THE MAKING OF WINNIE-THE-POOH

Ann Thwaite

With a preface by
Frank Cottrell-Boyce

St. Martin's Griffin ⚏ New York

GOODBYE CHRISTOPHER ROBIN. Copyright © 1990, 2017 by Ann Thwaite. Preface copyright © 2017 by Frank Cottrell-Boyce. All rights reserved. Printed in the United States of America. For information, address St. Martin's Press, 175 Fifth Avenue, New York, N.Y. 10010.

www.stmartins.com

The picture acknowledgements on page 255 constitute an extension of this copyright page.

The Library of Congress Cataloging-in-Publication Data is available upon request.

ISBN 978-1-250-19090-1 (trade paperback)
ISBN 978-1-250-19091-8 (ebook)

Our books may be purchased in bulk for promotional, educational, or business use. Please contact your local bookseller or the Macmillan Corporate and Premium Sales Department at 1-800-221-7945, extension 5442, or by email at MacmillanSpecialMarkets@macmillan.com.

First published in Great Britain under the title
A. A. Milne: His Life by Faber & Faber

Previously published in Great Britain as this abridged edition by Pan Books, an imprint of Pan Macmillan

First U.S. Edition: October 2017

10 9 8 7 6 5 4 3 2 1

For my dear daughters,
Emily, Caroline, Lucy and Alice,
with my love

CONTENTS

PREFACE

BY FRANK COTTRELL-BOYCE

Success simplifies.

Quentin Crisp famously pointed out in a lecture that if he were to bring a distinguished old Yorkshireman onto the stage, the audience might be perplexed. But if he brought a polished abstract sculpture with a hole in the middle, the audience would cry out, 'Ah! Henry Moore!' So A. A. Milne's long career as poet, playwright, polemicist, peace campaigner and novelist is completely eclipsed by four short children's books which – as he put it in 1952 – he created . . .

> . . . *little thinking*
> *All my years of pen-and-inking*
> *Would be almost lost among*
> *Those four trifles for the young.*

The only thing that's changed since 1952 is that 'almost' is no longer needed.

We are a society obsessed by the pursuit and adulation of success. We want to know The Secret of Your Success. And very very few things have been as successful as Winnie-the-Pooh. Pooh is one of those tiny handful of creations that are so enormously successful that we forget the infelicity of their name – Boots, The Beatles, Star Wars, Winnie-the-Pooh. There are many books that tell us how certain successes were or can be achieved – *How I Lost Weight / Became President / Won Gold – and How You Could Too*. But very few that tell us what success feels like, what lies in its aftermath. One of the great Secrets of Success is that more often than not it is not quite the kind of success you were hoping for. You want to be Hamlet but you're hailed as a clown. And now you can never be any kind of Hamlet. You want to move on but your global hit exerts all the gravity of a planet and you are trapped in its orbit. Failure at least has the comfort of hope. Milne's life story – as told here so compellingly by Ann Thwaite – brilliantly illuminates what it feels like to be tested by huge, unlooked-for success.

It isn't easy. Frankenstein was so eclipsed by his own creation that it has robbed him of his name. Milne had a long, successful career in the theatre – a world in which the writer gets used to a certain amount of petting and caressing. He gets to hear the audience call, 'Author! Author!' No one did that at Pooh events. They wanted to see the bear and – more troublingly – the boy. Milne isn't of course the only writer to find himself swallowed up by his own creation. You could say Milne's friend and hero J. M. Barrie wrote with great commercial success after *Peter Pan*, but what does 'after Peter Pan' mean? Peter Pan was, is and always will be. Barrie's other works are of their time. The over-arching drama of the Sherlock Holmes stories is the great detective's struggle, not with Moriarty, but with his own creator's attempts to kill him off.

Biography gives us the chance to restore some human complexity to the icon, to see some of the shade and shadow hidden behind the glare of monstrous success. Milne's career traces a path through the suave, seductive world of London clubs of the twenties, through the green rooms of Shaftesbury Avenue all the way up to the Disney section of the app store on my phone. It's good to be reminded of just how long and demanding an apprenticeship Milne had served before he discovered Pooh. His peerless dialogue has its roots in his playwriting career. His study of classics and his work on *Punch* had given him the extraordinary ease and range he shows in the poems. Milne's are probably the last poems written that really cry out to be memorised and recited. They float like a butterfly and sting like a bee. I can't think of a poem more easily absorbed and enjoyed than 'Disobedience'. I also can't think of one that captures so perfectly one of the true terrors of childhood.

It's good to be reminded, too, that Pooh was not universally adored, that writers who had admired Milne's lightness of touch turned on what they saw as the mawkishness of Pooh. 'Tonstant Weader', said Dorothy Parker, 'twowed up'. 'Timothy Bobbin', wrote P. G. Wodehouse, 'goes hoppity hoppity hoppity hoppity hop'. Cruellest of all is Richmal Crompton's brilliant skewering of the cult of Christopher Robin in the poem 'Homework' – 'Anthony Martin is doing his sums'.

The adulation of the public is salt in the wound of the writer who has lost the admiration of his peers.

One of the unexpected treasures of this book is Ann Thwaite's moving account of Milne's relationship with his brother Kenneth. Milne's letters to Kenneth uncover the well-spring of his creativity with all its childish joys, shadowed by tragedy. They are a real find. I was bewitched by this material when I read the book. Of course, when I was asked to write a film about Milne I left that out.

If success simplifies, film simplifies the simplification.

Or put another way, biography looks for what makes the individual different; drama looks for what we have in common. You can sell a million books if you write a good story well but a cultural phenomenon like Pooh needs something else. It needs to touch a raw nerve. That terrible review by Dorothy Parker also covered Christopher Morley's children's book *I Know a Secret* – which really is a pile of mawkish mush. There was a fashion for sentimentalising children on which people like Morley successfully cashed in. Milne on the other hand searched it for its source and found something true and terrible and enduring.

The House at Pooh Corner stands in a glade between two dark shadows – the aftermath of one war that had just finished and the dread of one coming. No one who fought in the First World War knew it was the First World War. On the contrary, they had been told that they were fighting the war that would end all wars. It must have been with the most bitter irony and failure, then, that that generation – Milne's generation – watched their children march away to a war that they had been told would never happen. The Milnes received that dreaded telegram telling them their son was missing in action and presumed he was dead. This can happen to anyone. This is feared by everyone. It's there – something you can build a film around. It's the shadow that makes the carefree days in the Hundred Acre Wood tremble and shimmer with their own fragility. They are suffused with a sense that happiness is possible and valid even though we know it is short-lived. It's a feeling that is expressed with peculiar intensity in the political situation of the between-the-war years but which applies to everyone, everywhere, all the time.

It is there, too, in the child who plays in the woods – in Christopher Robin himself. On the one hand he is Robin Hood revelling in the freedom of the Greenwood but he's also a babe lost in the wood. What marks Christopher Robin out from other children in literature – from William, say – is that he's often absent from the adventures. Often his role is to come and put things right. He's more like a kindly uncle than a child. Through the carefree forest he carries a burden of responsibility.

The other unusual thing about Christopher Robin of course is that he was – to some extent – a real boy. It also swallowed Christopher Robin. The difference between Winnie-the-Pooh and, say, Sherlock Holmes, is that Pooh did not just swallow Milne. Imagine if Barrie had called Peter Pan Peter Llewelyn Davies. When Czeslaw Milosz said, 'When a writer is born into a family, the family is finished', he meant that a writer will betray his parents and siblings. Milne on the other hand – however innocently – betrayed his son. The magic of the Hundred Acre Wood is that it takes something painfully fleeting and makes it stay for ever. The tragedy of Milne's success is that it trapped a real child in that moment like a fly in amber and made it almost impossible for him to become that thing that every child wants to become – a grown-up. Is there a threat more pathetic and painful than Christopher Robin's cry, 'We'll see how father likes it when I write poems about HIM.'

It's a complex, nuanced story and it takes this whole book to unpack it. But it's worth pointing out that what abides of this story – what moves us – is the happiness and beauty that Milne rescued from it. I've used the word 'aftermath' a couple of times in this preface. Aftermath nowadays is almost always used to refer to damage and ruin but its original meaning is the second harvest that is sometimes possible after the first has been gathered in. For all its shadow, what really abides about this story is the light, the sense that happiness – no matter how fleeting – is real. The fact that we are all moved and enchanted by the Hundred Acre Wood, that it calls to us, is proof that these passing moments are as real and essential as the more solid and enduring things with which we surround ourselves, that we find in them something true and paradoxically enduring, even eternal.

As R. S. Thomas put it in his poem 'The Bright Field':

> *It is the turning*
> *aside like Moses to the miracle*
> *of the lit bush, to a brightness*
> *that seemed as transitory as your youth*
> *once, but is the eternity that awaits you.*

INTRODUCTION

I have often been asked how I came to write about A. A. Milne and his son, Christopher Robin. After my second biography, *Edmund Gosse: A Literary Landscape*, won a prize, I was approached by a number of publishers and A. A. Milne was one of the suggestions. He seemed particularly appropriate for a biographer who had just written about another complex father–son relationship; and before that about Frances Hodgson Burnett, whose son, Vivian, had inspired *Little Lord Fauntleroy*. In 1974 the *Observer* called Christopher Robin 'the most famous of all tiny boys (by comparison Little Lord Fauntleroy was a mere starlet)'.

It was also relevant that I had myself been brought up on A. A. Milne. My father had given *Winnie-the-Pooh* to my mother when it first came out in 1926, six years before I was born. I knew many of the poems and stories by heart. My own London childhood had been a slightly downmarket version of Christopher Robin's. We did not have a country cottage, but we did have a stream, the Dollis Brook, at the bottom of our north London garden. Even my double name (I was always called Ann Barbara as a child) had more to do with Christopher Robin than with Princess Margaret Rose.

When A. A. Milne came up as a possible subject for me, I felt it likely that Christopher Milne would turn me down, as I knew he had rejected others. He had himself written two memoirs and had actually said in the second one, *The Path Through the Trees*, that the first one, *The Enchanted Places*, was written to forestall strangers. But I knew I could only write about this father and son if I had his approval and permission to quote any relevant material.

I was elated when Christopher said not only that he was prepared to let me write the book, but that I must write it as if he were not going to read it. When, after the long years of research and writing, I gave him his copy of the finished book, he eventually wrote to tell me that 'if I had any doubts and reluctance at the beginning, they have all been swept away and I am left with nothing but admiration and happiness.' His reaction was a great relief to both of us.

A. A. Milne: His Life was published in 1990, on both sides of the Atlantic, and won the Whitbread Prize for the best biography of the year. It went into a number of editions and is now available from Pan Macmillan as an ebook and as a print-on-demand paperback. *Goodbye Christopher Robin* is not just a cut version of the biography. It is the full story of how A. A. Milne came to write the four great children's books and how Christopher Robin became one of the most famous children in the world. It is a story of celebrity and of the joys and pains of success.

Christopher Milne died in 1996 after what he himself called a happy life. I don't know whether he would have been surprised at the new twenty-first-century surge of interest in *Winnie-the-Pooh*. Recently the book came top in a BBC poll to find the best children's book ever. In 2017 there is a grand exhibition devoted to Winnie-the-Pooh at the Victoria and Albert Museum in London. And best of all, because it can be seen all over the world, in all the countries where the books have been translated, there will be the remarkable film produced by Damian Jones, directed by Simon Curtis and written by Frank Cottrell-Boyce. This is the story behind that film.

May, 2017

GOODBYE
CHRISTOPHER ROBIN

❧

BEFORE YOU BEGIN

Alan Alexander Milne was born on 18 January 1882, the much-loved youngest of the three sons of a schoolmaster called John Vine Milne and his wife, Maria. Both his parents were of what one might call humble origin. They had made their own ways in the world. Alan Milne grew up at Henley House, a small private school in a part of London Milne would call 'the Kilburn end of Maida Vale'. Five minutes' walk away, in what he would call St John's Wood, lived a boy, born just over two years earlier, who would grow up to be Milne's illustrator, E. H. Shepard. Their names would be permanently linked, but they did not meet until years later in the new century, when they both worked for *Punch*, described then as the most famous humorous paper in the world.

Henley House was a good school and Alan flourished as his father's pupil. He and his next brother, Ken, enjoyed an extraordinary amount of freedom when they were quite small. The wide open spaces of Hampstead Heath were not far away for boys with bicycles. It is no wonder that there are no nannies or nursery rules in the Enchanted Forest. Pooh and his friends are the children who explore a world where only friendship and hunger and the desire for adventure affect the pattern of their days and a boy called Christopher Robin plays the role of the wise and helpful parent with whom the listening or reading child identifies.

A very clever child, at eleven Alan Milne won a scholarship to Westminster School and joined Ken there. He would, in the far future, remember the school with gratitude, but, after one unjust, crushing report, he said that he 'turned to the lighter side of life and abandoned work'.

Certainly he gave up any mathematical ambitions but he still managed to win a minor scholarship to Trinity College, Cambridge, and, more importantly, had already developed a talent for light verse.

At Cambridge, Milne edited *Granta*, the university magazine. He began to hone the skills that, not long after leaving Cambridge, got him a place on the staff of *Punch* at a point when he said he had only £2 in his bank account. He was appointed assistant editor in 1906, aged twenty-four. He had already by then published one book (a collection of related stories he later disowned), a great deal of journalism and had written several unperformed plays. Now he had a good salary and 100,000 readers every week.

Even before the success of his plays, A. A. Milne was becoming something of a celebrity. Invitations poured in, often from people he didn't really know. *The Day's Play*, a collection of his *Punch* pieces, was a bestseller. The *Daily Graphic* painted a vivid picture of families up and down the land tearing *Punch* apart in their eagerness to read what Milne had written. He found himself being compared with Lewis Carroll, though children were hardly yet part of the picture.

In January 1913, he went to Switzerland on a skiing holiday, found Daphne de Sélincourt, god-daughter of his editor, was staying at the same hotel and returned to London engaged to marry her. They married at St Margaret's, Westminster, on 4 June that same year. It was the day of the Derby when Emily Davis threw herself in front of the King's horse and died. Daphne was not a suffragette, though she had agreed with Alan that the word 'obey' in the marriage service meant only that she would 'write all my thank-you-very-much letters for me'.

Christopher Milne would one day explain why his

parents married – a marriage that seems to need some explanation, as many marriages do – in a phrase his father had used himself: 'She laughed at my jokes'.

Daphne, highly polished and glamorous as she was, came from a very different background – wealthy trade with yachts and fast cars. She had no interest in politics. The way things looked were always of more concern to her. Alan Milne himself was a passionate democrat who canvassed for the Liberals, street by street, in the close-run 1910 elections. He was a pacifist.

In a letter to his American publisher, he would one day write:

> *You have always told me that personally you have always thought more of* Winnie-the-Pooh *than any book I have ever written. Please let me tell you that I think more of* Peace with Honour *than any book I have ever written.*

This bestselling pacifist tract was not published until 1934, but Milne had called himself a pacifist since 1910 and the seeds of this serious and important book were inevitably in his mind throughout the war and in the twenties, as he suffered from his ghastly experiences on the Somme.

The war shattered the world that Milne had written

about in *Punch*, as it shattered so much else, and so many lives. In his autobiography, Milne wrote, 'It makes me almost physically sick to think of that nightmare of mental and moral degradation, the war.' It is difficult for us to understand, after the killing of one Archduke had led to the deaths of 'ten million men who were not arch-dukes', just how widely the war was welcomed in 1914. Milne himself briefly felt it might be 'the war that will end war', in his friend H. G. Wells' phrase that would become a sad cliché. He hoped that the war might make people realise the true futility of war, but on the Somme he came to know it as 'a lunacy which would shame the madhouse'.

The talk of 'shirkers' and white feathers in the *Punch* office was intolerable. Milne finally volunteered in February 1915. 'Life in wartime is hell anyway. And only in uniform can one escape thinking about it,' he said, illogically. In March he was commissioned into the War-wickshire Regiment stationed at Golden Hill Fort on the Isle of Wight. Much later, Milne was able to record that in the entire war he had never fired a shot in anger or even in defence. The reason for this (which soothed his pacifist conscience) was that he had volunteered for a nine-week course at the Southern Command Signalling School at Wyke Regis, near Weymouth. On his return to the Isle of Wight he was registered as 'Indispensable to the Training of the Battalion'. He was lucky, as so often in life. 'Had I not been a Signals Officer, I should have gone out in July and the second battalion was wiped out to a man, or rather to an officer, in the advance.' Daphne joined him on the island and they were able to rent a cottage in Sandown.

It was there in the winter of 1915–16 that Milne wrote the first play of his that was actually performed – written partly to give the five children of his Colonel something to do and partly to amuse himself and Daphne (who took it down from his dictation and appeared in it as the Wicked Countess) 'at a time when life was not very amusing'. The script has not survived, but it was the germ of Milne's first children's book, *Once on a Time*. That was first published in 1917, with a later edition, illustrated by Charles Robinson, appearing five years later, not long before *When We Were Very Young*.

Daily expecting to be sent to France to replace a Signals officer who had been killed, Milne just had time, in the evenings of his days training new recruits, to write another play. It had to be a comedy, with nothing whatsoever to do with the war. This was the strangely named *Wurzel Flummery*. Reduced to two acts, it would eventually be his first West End production in a bill with two short plays by his friend J. M. Barrie.

Alan Milne arrived on the Somme in the summer of 1916, at a time when, after the initial slaughter (nearly 20,000 British soldiers killed and 40,000 wounded on the first day alone), 10,000 more were killed or wounded every day that passed. The young subaltern with whom Milne had travelled out was killed within a week. It was horrific. Even in July they were fighting in a field of mud, among smashed and leafless trees and half-buried bodies. The stench and the flies were appalling. Milne ran out his first wire on 11 August. It was dangerous work trying to keep the lines of communication open.

There were few breaks in the horror. Milne longed for 'a nice cushy wound' to take him away from it. In the end, it was a serious case of trench fever, with a temperature soaring to 105°F, that took him back to England, to a hospital in Oxford and eventually to a convalescent home at Osborne on the Isle of Wight. It has been said that Milne had a quiet war. No one who spent any time on the Somme had a quiet war. On the Somme it was only quiet if you were dead. The bombardment and the buzzing flies, feeding on the dead, sounded in his ears for years. But he knew how lucky he was to be alive and, having been in it, have a greater right to speak out against the lunacy of war.

A medical board recommended sedentary work. Milne was still not well when he started in Intelligence, based at the War Office. The work was secret and included in 1918 a mysterious visit to France, but most of the time he was in London, living with Daphne again. Every moment now that the Army left him alone, Milne was writing plays. After *Wurzel Flummery* came *Belinda*, *The Boy Comes Home*, *Make-Believe* (for children), *The Camberley Triangle* and *The Lucky One*. These are plays that are now forgotten, though they attracted much attention and gave a good deal of pleasure at the time. All were written, astonishingly, while Milne was still in the Army.

Belinda opened on 8 April 1918. On the day it was reviewed in *The Times*, a leader reported the renewal of the German offensive. Four hundred thousand more men died in three weeks. *Belinda* survived London's worst air raid of the war and was taken off after nine weeks. 'It was difficult,' Milne said, 'to regard its ill fortune as a matter of much importance.'

Milne was finally demobilised on Valentine's Day in 1919. He had always expected to return to *Punch* after the war. Daphne had dreamed that Alan would succeed Sir Owen Seaman, her godfather, as editor and be knighted like him. It was a shock that he was not wanted back as assistant editor. It was presumed he would much prefer to write plays. The fact was that to Sir Owen, Milne was, as he had always been, too liberal, too 'radical'. Milne found it hard, some hurt would remain, but he was getting tired of London and he was optimistic that the play he was writing would be the one to make his fortune.

NOW READ ON . . .

I

PLAYWRIGHT

In 1922, the year A. A. Milne was forty and two years before the first of the famous children's books was published, a caption to his photograph in a London newspaper carried the words: 'Milne came to Fleet Street years ago in search of a fortune. As a dramatist, his income at times ranges from £200 to £500 a week.' This really was a fortune in 1922; it was more in a week than most people earned in a year. That joking boast, 'England's premier playwright', which Alan Milne had used when signing a letter to his brother Ken in 1917, was never exactly justified. But he was certainly one of England's most successful, prolific and best-known playwrights for a brief period, a fact that now seems almost incredible, when so many people who know his name and love his books have no idea that he ever wrote plays.

It was in 1919 that A. A. Milne had joined the Garrick

Club. The club was to give him a great deal of pleasure (a refuge, another home, particularly in the thirties) – pleasure he would reward on his death with a share of the Pooh royalties. The Garrick was the appropriate club for a playwright. The Garrick was full of actors; it was full of writers too.

Milne in 1919 was ambitious, and not just to make a lot of money. Towards the end of his life, he summed up his feelings like this:

> Of all the foolish things which Dr Johnson said, the most foolish was: 'No man but a blockhead ever wrote, except for money.' What he should have said was that a writer, having written what pleased him, was a blockhead if he did not sell it in the best market. But a writer wants something more than money for his work: he wants permanence ... He yearns for the immortality, even if only in the British Museum, of stiff covers.

Milne made sure that most of his plays were published in an attractive uniform edition from Chatto and Windus, in a stylish brown cloth with a well-designed label on the spine. 'It is very jolly indeed,' he told his novelist friend and editor Frank Swinnerton, when he saw the proofs of *First Plays*. Twenty of Milne's plays survive in this form, and not only in the British Museum. But the true immortality was to come, of course, from the children's books, a fact he would live to realise and regret.

The play that was Milne's first real success was *Mr Pim Passes By*, which opened at the New Theatre in London on 5 January 1920. It was a hard audience to woo. The great successes of the 1920s were *Chu Chin Chow* and *Hassan*, glamorous and specifically exotic musical shows, which fulfilled to perfection people's need for a good night out. In the straight theatre, the playwright's best hope was to make people laugh. He also had to remember all sorts of practical things. Theatres were less well-disciplined places than they usually are today. 'If yours is an 8.15 play, you may be sure that the stalls will not fill up till 8.30 and you should therefore let loose the lesser-paid members of the cast in the opening scene.' You should be careful not to waste your jokes 'on the first five pages of dialogue'. There would be a crackle of stiff white shirtfronts, a jingle of beaded evening bags, a shuffle of programmes as the audience settled themselves into their seats. And at the end of the evening the playwright had to remember that many people, living for instance in Chislehurst, would be catching last trains and missing the final five minutes of every play they ever saw, together, of course, with countless renderings of the national anthem.

There was a more personal problem. The Milnes were becoming worried at Daphne's failure to conceive. They both wanted children. They had now been married for nearly six years; the war had not kept them apart for any great periods of time. There were consultations with a gynaecologist. In May 1919, Daphne went into a nursing home. 'I fly there in all my spare minutes,' Milne wrote to Swinnerton, adding that he was trying to write a novel called *Nocturne*, but kept putting it aside. The operation Daphne underwent was 'officially' for the removal of her appendix, but it seems likely that something else was done at the same time; perhaps the fallopian tubes were insufflated. Whatever happened, in April 1920 J. M. Barrie would be able to congratulate Milne: 'By far the choicest lines (the best you have ever written) are about your wife and I rejoice with exceeding joy over that news.' Daphne was expecting a child in August.

The nursery was ready. They had moved into 'the prettiest little house in London', Milne wrote to Frank Swinnerton in August 1919, describing 11 Mallord Street, Chelsea, SW3. It is a short, quiet street just a few minutes' walk from the King's Road.

The house is narrow, in a terrace, and had been built

not long before the war. It has three storeys and a basement and is much bigger than it looks from outside, having been designed rather cleverly round a well for light. The house was much described in the late 1920s, when hordes of journalists traipsed through it on their way to Christopher Robin's nursery. 'Originally Mallord Street had been done in colours influenced by the Russian Ballet, black carpets, bright cushions, very impractical as the carpets showed every bit of cigarette ash,' a friend of Daphne's remembered her saying. 'She told me that the thing to be at that time was – different.' The house had to be 'an artistic whole, a showplace'.

Some of Milne's own exuberant pleasure in his new house comes across in a piece he published in the *Sphere* on 9 August 1919, soon after they moved in. It was the first time, he said, that he had had the chance to go upstairs to bed and come downstairs to breakfast for nineteen years – in other words since he had left home for Cambridge.

Of course I have done these things in other people's houses from time to time, but what we do in other people's houses does not count ... Now, however, for the first time in nineteen years, I am actually living in a house. I have (imagine my excitement) a staircase of my own.

Flats may be convenient (I thought so myself when I lived in one some days ago), but they have their disadvantages. One of the disadvantages is that you are never in complete possession of the flat. You may think that the drawing-room floor (to take a case) is your very own, but it isn't; you share it with a man below who uses it as a ceiling. If you want to dance a stepdance, you have to consider his plaster. I was always ready enough to accommodate myself in this matter to his prejudices, but I could not put up with his old-fashioned ideas about bathroom ceilings. It is very cramping to one's style in the bath to reflect that the slightest splash may call attention to itself on the ceiling of the gentleman below. This is to share a bathroom with a stranger – an intolerable position for a proud man. Today I have a bathroom of my own for the first time in my life.

I can see already that living in a house is going to be extraordinarily healthy both for mind and body. At present I go upstairs to my bedroom (and downstairs again) about once in every half-hour. No such exercise as this was possible in a flat, and even after two or three days I feel the better for it.

But the best of a house is that it has an outside personality as well as an inside one. Any of you may find himself some day in our quiet street, and stop a moment to look at our house; at the blue door with its jolly knocker, at the little trees in their blue tubs standing within a ring of blue posts linked by chains, at the bright-coloured curtains. We have the pleasure of feeling that we are contributing something to London. We are part of a street now, and can take pride in that street.

That being 'part of a street' was not quite as community-minded a remark as it suggests, although Milne would become friends with some people who lived nearby. Harold Fraser-Simson, the composer, had a house across the street and belonged to the Garrick Club. W. A. Darlington and his family lived only a few minutes' walk away. They would all see each other from time to time. Darlington described his first visit:

As I rang the bell of his house in Mallord Street I was attacked by a fit of shyness. I had admired his work so deeply and for so long that I had a sudden absurd feeling that I was a fag in the lower fourth who had been sent for by a member of the upper sixth. This vanished the moment I met him. Milne in the flesh was all I had hoped to find him, warm, friendly and amusing.

Milne had invited Darlington to call. Darlington's review of *Mr Pim Passes By* was written on the night of the confirmation of his appointment as drama critic of the *Daily Telegraph*, a job he was to hold for the rest of his career. The Milnes were not callers. 'We don't call very well,' Milne said. 'My fault, I suppose. I hate knowing people for geographical reasons.' Their neighbours felt the same. When the Milnes were burgled, the people next door sent a note of sympathy. Even then they did not speak to each other. 'Suburban chumminess' never appealed to Milne. Already he felt it necessary to protect his privacy. But he was not always consistent. Milne once said to Swinnerton: 'Does any person think so consecutively and business-likely as novelists make them think?' Real people are never as consistent as the characters in fiction. Milne could be said, at some points, to have been someone who kept himself to himself. On other days, in other moods, he would welcome the warm curiosity, the genuine interest of a fellow human being.

The one generalisation which always does seem to be true of Milne – unfashionable and indeed repugnant as some people find it – can best be left in Frank Swinnerton's own words, the words of someone who knew him really well. 'He loves goodness . . . He stands for virtue.' He had been brought up to believe that, without virtue, nothing is worth anything. This does not mean, of course, that he always himself did the right thing but rather that he had a strong moral sense. Swinnerton saw this as a problem for Milne professionally. 'He combined with a gift for persiflage the sternness of a Covenanter, which I think restricted the range of his dramatic performance. Any writer of imaginative work who cannot give the Devil his due ... becomes moral-bound. He dare not let sinners have a flutter.' 'Rectitude is fatal to humour,' Graham Greene would say, hitting Milne when he was already down, in the 1930s. The redeeming fact was that Milne's admiration was for real goodness, not for those Victorian virtues, or indeed 'the prevailing social codes' which so often pass as such. But it would, as we shall see, earn him some dislike. Those who stand for goodness risk being called prudish, priggish and proud. 'I felt uncomfortable in his company,' one of his publishers told me. 'Those who disagree with him complain of his rigidity in argument and severity in outlook,' Swinnerton said, adding, 'That is not my experience. I have always found him overflowing with good spirits.'

Alan Milne's parents, who had now sold their school and retired, were living in the war years and just after in a house called St Andrews at Burgess Hill in Sussex. One of Alan's nieces, Angela, remembered: 'To a child from suburbia, St Andrews was heaven.' It was 'a compact Victorian country house, brick, gabled, with a squat tower', standing in its own grounds. There was Pears' soap in the bathroom, a grandfather clock in the hall, stone lions and passion-flowers at the front door. Maria by now was ailing, moving only slowly round the house, with a stick, a shawl and a lace cap. She taught her grandchildren a moral verse, as she must have taught her own children, thirty years before.

> For every evil under the sun
> There is a remedy or there is none.
> If there is one, try and find it;
> If there isn't one, never mind it.

'J. V. Milne was more sprightly, a small man (he got smaller with age) with a neat white beard and a panama hat. He wore pince-nez and showed his Scottishness by pronouncing "grass" with a short "a" . . . He would stroll round the garden (hands behind back) with us, telling us useful and funny things.' The garden was full of frogs and apples. The house often resounded to 'Trumpeter, what are you trumpeting now?' on the gramophone and to Harry Lauder singing 'I Love a Lassie'.

The elderly Milnes' great source of pride and pleasure

was, of course, A. A. Milne's rise to fame and fortune. Alan had given his father a subscription to the General Press Cutting Association Ltd, as early as 1910, and J. V. stuck the cuttings neatly into a stout black notebook. Before long there would be productions of Milne plays all over the place in little theatres and community playhouses. In the west of England, two boys who would grow up to be Charles Causley, the poet, and J. C. Trewin, the drama critic, would both remember *Mr Pim Passes By* as their first happy experience of the theatre.

It ran in London for 246 performances and opened in New York for another successful run on 28 February 1921. For the rest of Milne's life it would continue to make him money. Milne had had a sort of fame for years as a *Punch* humorist. Now the morning post increased dramatically. He was much in demand. Photographers wrote wanting to photograph him. 'Very handsome, long-headed, keen-faced', as Swinnerton described him, he looks out from dozens of photographs taken in the 1920s.

Milne himself was writing his novel based on the play. 'I know very little about the writing of novels – or the writing of plays for that matter – but I hope I am learning. And, anyway, it is much more fun trying to do things which you can't quite do than doing them when you can.' The novel, *Mr Pim*, included most of the dialogue from the play, but it was 'a real book', Milne said, 'and not just the dialogue with "he said" or "she said" tacked on.' The idea had not been Milne's own, but it worked extremely well.

Milne had already finished another novel, a detective story, *The Red House Mystery*, though it would not be published until 1922, after *Mr Pim*. He said, modestly, much later: 'The result would have passed unnoticed in these days when so many good writers are writing so many good detective stories, but in those days there was not so much competition.' It was actually written just before the publication of Agatha Christie's first book *The Mysterious Affair at Styles* (a book which, thirty years later, he would call 'the model detective story') and published a year before Dorothy Sayers's first novel. In an introduction to a later edition of *The Red House Mystery* Milne comments on his agents' lack of enthusiasm for the new project. He was, after all, typecast as a humorist. But it was in Milne's nature, and demonstrated throughout his career, to refuse to be typecast. It was always more interesting to try something new. 'It has been my good fortune as a writer that what I have wanted to write has for the most part proved to be saleable. It has been my misfortune as a businessman that, when it has proved to be extremely saleable, then I have not wanted to write it any more.' This would be true in turn of humorous essays, detective stories and children's books.

A. A. Milne had an enviable confidence in his own activities. His niece, Angela, remembered Milne telling her 'that he had a superiority complex; not boasting, or confessing, simply stating a fact. I am sure it was true,' she said. 'All Milnes have been brought up to believe that never mind about money . . . it's BRAINS THAT COUNT.' It would be poor Pooh's lack of brain that would cause most of his problems and give Christopher Robin (and the listening child) that delightful feeling of superiority that Milne enjoyed so much of the time, even if, occasionally, it was accompanied by intolerance and impatience. Friends and acquaintances could find this very difficult, though he often managed to cloak it with a becoming, self-mocking modesty. With his strong conviction of his own worth, there went a sad inability to accept criticism. W. A. Darlington put it like this:

Alan and I spent most of our time together on various golf courses, where we had, or soon acquired, a number of mutual friends. It was from these that I learned the disconcerting fact that, devoted to Alan as they were, they all found him on occasion very difficult to deal with. The trouble was, I was told, that he simply could not take any form of adverse criticism. 'Say the wrong thing to him,' I was warned, 'and he freezes stone cold and won't speak to you for the rest of the day.'

It is not an uncommon trait in the creative artist to desire praise and shrink from censure, but Alan evidently had it to an abnormal degree. The violence of his reaction against even a hint of blame had in it something pathological, as if he were short of a skin.

Was it perhaps that he had never needed in his glowing cherished childhood to grow any form of protective coating? Long ago there was the blow of a first bad Westminster report for the boy who had spent his early years as the headmaster's beloved youngest son, the child so lapped in love and admiration that he thought he could do anything. Milne had, indeed, as many writers have, an intense need for praise. He once wrote about 'that sense of inspiration and power that only comes upon me after violent praise'. And, on another occasion, when asked by an interviewer whether Daphne, so often at this period still involved in taking his dictation, ever criticised what he had written at the end of the day, he said, 'No, she just praises ... Praise is what an author really wants when he is actually writing.' It was, in fact, what he always wanted.

2

THE ARRIVAL OF
CHRISTOPHER ROBIN

In the summer of 1920 Daphne Milne gave birth to their first and only son in the house in Chelsea. It was not an easy birth. Daphne told a friend long afterwards about it. 'It's difficult to believe,' the friend said to me, 'but until she was actually giving birth, she had no idea of the mechanics of it. It came as a thoroughly traumatising shock and made her absolutely determined never to repeat the performance.' It is not so difficult to believe. In Milne's novel *Two People*, the wife says her mother had told her absolutely nothing before she was married – nothing about anything. Not many young women had yet read *Married Love* by Marie Stopes, published only two years earlier.

It seems likely, from clues in his fiction, that Alan Milne was the traditional anguished husband, pacing up and down through the hours of labour, in a room not far away, pulling on his pipe. 'Because his son had been so long in coming, he had been more than usually frightened,' Milne wrote in a late short story. 'He looked at his son, and felt as other husbands have felt looking at their first-born, "All that for this; so small, so ugly; and yet what a burden to have borne."' Another of his characters says, 'When my boy was born, we lived in two rooms. Mary was in one; I was in the other.' He heard the birth. 'It was not for me to say how many children we should have.' '"I can't bear to think of your being frightened and ill and so terribly hurt," he cried out, in sudden shame of himself, of his sex, of all that women have suffered from men.' And in his own voice, A. A. Milne said clearly: 'To me, the miracle of Human Birth is more worthy of awe than the miracle of Virgin Birth . . . What a piece of work is a man!'

Christopher Robin Milne was born on 21 August 1920 and so registered, but he was to be known immediately as Billy and later Moon – from his own pronunciation of Milne. On the 22nd, his father wrote to Frank Swinnerton:

> *A tremendous event has happened, unrecked of by the minor novelist. THERE IS A JUNIOR MILNE! This is a creation of my wife's (Daff*

– short for Daphne or, as some say, Daffodil) and before it the trumpery creations of the aforesaid minor novelists pale their ineffectual fires. (Shakespeare, or one of those people.) Locally this creation is known as Billy.

Sir, if you never grovelled before, grovel now in the presence of this miracle. When women can do these things, why do we go on writing, you and I? (You observe that I put us both on one level, but I am in a generous mood this evening.) Why do we continue to call ourselves lords of creation when we so obviously are not? Why – but I must not overtax your brain!

Salute Chatto for me, slap Windus on the back. Tell them to mark August 21st in letters of blood on their calendars. And believe me to be, Sir,

Your mental superior

A. A. Milne

who shines equally as Husband, Father, Citizen and Author.

He wrote rather more soberly a few days later to Biddie Warren, a friend of his parents, in reply to her congratulations: 'Daff and Billy (to be Christopher Robin but called Billy) are both extremely well. He weighed ten pounds or so the Nurse said, but I suspect that Nurses are rather like fishermen, and he has lots of curly brown hair, and not a bad little face for his age. We did rather want a Rosemary, but I expect we shall be just as happy with this gentleman.' J. M. Barrie wrote: 'All my heartiest congratulations to you both, or strictly speaking to the three of you. May Billy be an everlasting joy to you. From what you say I gather he is already a marvel, but I shall decide about this for myself when I see him, which I hope will be soon.'

There has grown up a definite idea, encouraged by Milne's own need to distance himself from his children's books, that A. A. Milne was not particularly interested in children or good with them. He wrote in his autobiography in 1939, at a time when he most wanted to remind his readers that he was a writer, not just a children's writer: 'I am not inordinately fond of or interested in children; their appeal to me is a physical appeal such as the young of other animals make. I have never felt in the least sentimental about them, or no more sentimental than one becomes for a moment over a puppy or a kitten. In as far as I understand their minds the understanding is based on the observation, casual enough and mostly unconscious, which I give to people generally: on memories of my own childhood: and on the imagination

which every writer must bring to the memory and observation.' He had both remembered and observed, he said,
'the uncharming part of a child's nature: the egotism and
the heartlessness'.

The idea of the children's writer who does not like
children is a paradox that seems to lodge in people's
minds – minds that are nowadays often rather suspicious
of Lewis Carroll's delight in little girls. Peter Green
gave wide circulation to the idea that Milne was uneasy
with children in his biography of Kenneth Grahame,
though all the evidence is that Milne did not share
Grahame's habit of ignoring them. People often say:
'Oh, A. A. Milne? He didn't like children, did he?' It is
the thing they think they 'know' about him. Christopher
Milne's own memoir of his childhood is presumably
largely responsible. He wrote: 'Some people are good
with children. Others are not. It is a gift. You either have
it or you don't. My father didn't – not with children, that
is. Later on it was different, very different. But I am
thinking of nursery days.'

It is certainly difficult to dispute the evidence of the
child himself. But all the letters of those nursery years
suggest that Milne, if not in the simplest sense 'good with
children', was always intensely interested in his son and
not just far more observant (a natural corollary of the fact

of being a writer who had always drawn on the world around him), but much more involved in his son's life than the great majority of fathers of the period.

There is hardly a letter of Milne's surviving from his son's childhood which does not mention the child, and very often he sent photographs as well. ('Which one is Billy?' asked J. M. Barrie, looking at two unidentified babies in October 1921. 'I'll come and find out. Don't tell me.') The reviews of Christopher's autobiography all picked up the same impression as the *Daily Mail*: 'The Christopher Robin of the stories scarcely knew the busy writer who was his father.' That was what Christopher himself thought, looking back fifty years later: 'If I cannot say that I loved my parents, it is only because, in those early days, I just didn't know them well enough.' Christopher may not think he knew his father, but his father certainly knew him. From the very beginning the child dominated the household. Inviting Edward Marsh to lunch to meet him (and 'that great actress Athene Seyler'), Milne names the time as one-thirty. 'It has to be 1.30, because Billy insists on his lunch at 1.' He was then two months old. The following June J. V. Milne, the child's grandfather, wrote to a friend: 'Alan says he spends too much time with Billy, seeing all the work before him.'

Long before Christopher was born, there is plenty of

evidence that Milne, unlike Daphne, really knew about babies. There was a child-centred series in *Punch* called 'The Heir', at the time of the birth of his brother Ken's first son, which again shows Milne in his most characteristic attitude to children: fascinated but totally unsentimental.

Dahlia gushes about her infant. He is the living image of his father: 'I looked closely at Archie and then at the baby. "I should always know them apart," I said at last.' Milne shows a confident superiority when Samuel, a godfather, who knows nothing about children, bestows an enormous teddy on his tiny godson, saying 'I've been calling it Duncan on the train, but of course he will want to choose his own name for it.' He expects a ridiculous amount from the child. 'Is he tall for his age?' he asks. 'Samuel, pull yourself together. He isn't tall at all; if he is anything he is long but how long only those can say who have seen him in his bath. You do realise that he is only a month old?' 'My dear old boy, of course . . . I suppose he isn't even toddling?' 'No, no,' Milne says, 'Not actually toddling.'

'We did rather want a Rosemary,' Milne said in that early letter. One of his son's earliest memories would be of a time when he was still small enough to be in a pram. Relaxing outside a grocer's shop in Chelsea, he heard someone say, 'Oh what a pretty little girl!' Like his father before him, he would have to wait a long time for his first haircut. His long hair reminded his mother of the girl she'd wanted and his father of the boy he himself had been. Christopher Milne would remember: 'I had long hair at a time when boys didn't have long hair . . . I used to wear girlish clothes, too, smocks and things. And in my very earliest dreams I even used to dream I was a girl.' The child's image was 'surely Daff, not Alan', one of his cousins commented. Milne himself, looking at the long-haired child in the pretty clothes, must have remembered his own childish feelings of 'battling against the wrong make-up'. Perhaps he thought if it hadn't done him much harm (and indeed, as he suggested, had made him the sort of person he was, the sort of writer he was) then it would not do Billy much harm either.

Alan had felt himself bold and brave under his girlish disguise. His son, on the other hand, suggests image and reality were more closely related in his case. There was not much battling going on. He was content to be gentle, shy and quiet. W. A. Darlington remembers 'a nice little boy . . . being brought up on rather soft and effeminate lines'. His own daughter, Anne, eight months or so older, a tougher character, became the boy's closest friend. They were 'devoted and almost inseparable – Anne with a slight touch about her of the elder sister.' And Alan and

Daphne were equally devoted to Anne: 'Anne was and remained to her death the Rosemary that I wasn't,' Christopher Milne would write.

At least with a boy there is the chance to dream of him playing cricket for England. Years before, Milne had said that 'the important thing in christening a future first-class cricketer is to get the initials right'. Christopher Robin was, in fact, never christened, but his names were undoubtedly something to do with having the right sort of initials. 'What could be better than W. G. as a nickname for Grace? But if W. G.'s initials had been Z. Z. where would you have been?' Years later Milne wrote:

When Christopher Robin was born, he had to have a name. We had already decided to call him something else and later on he decided to call himself something still else, so that the two names for which we were now looking were to be no more than an excuse for giving him two initials for use in later life. I had decided on two initials rather than one or none, because I wanted him to play cricket for England, like W. G. Grace and C. B. Fry, and if he was to play as an amateur, two initials would give him a more hopeful appearance on the score-card. A father has to think of these things. So, one of us liking the name Christopher, and the other maintaining that Robin was both pleasing and unusual, we decided that as C. R. Milne he should be encouraged to make his name in the sporting world.

There was no idea yet, of course, that it would be his father who would make his name for him, by using those names which he never used himself and which seemed to have so little to do with him – so that there would come a time when, not C. R. Milne, but Christopher Robin, could be described as one of the 'five most famous children in the world'. Long afterwards the child himself would write of the fairy who must have pronounced over his cradle 'one of those cryptic spells that fairies had always been good at: "And his name shall be famous throughout the world." It was one of those spells that sound like a blessing but turn out to be more like a curse.'

In the meantime, his father pondered on the fact that there were still four years to go before Billy could possibly have his first cricket lesson, and got on with his next play. This stage of Milne's life would undoubtedly become tedious to the reader if all sixteen of A. A. Milne's plays, short and long, which were produced in the 1920s, were examined in detail. But there were landmarks and highlights which cannot be ignored. There were recurrent excitements and recurrent disappointments. 'Plays always

go well on a first night,' Milne would suggest in his novel
Two People, 'and then the critics tell you why you didn't
really enjoy it as much as you thought you did, and how
much nicer it would have been if someone else had written quite a different one.'

In 1921 they were able to leave Billy and enjoy a month in
Italy without worrying, for they now had the perfect nurse
for him – Olive Rand – whom her charge would always
call 'Nou', but who would become known to the world
as Alice, because of a happy rhyme with Palace. ('They're
changing guard at Buckingham Palace / Christopher
Robin went down with Alice . . .') 'The English mother
is fortunate,' said Daphne Milne in an interview in New
York in 1931, forgetting all the English mothers who
weren't. 'The English mother is fortunate in being able to
place such full confidence in her children's nurse. Often
the trusted and beloved "Nanny" remains in the employ
of the family for years . . . She is especially trained for her
work, which she regards as a real profession, worthy of
her pride and deepest interest.'

Olive Rand would remain with the Milnes until
Christopher went to boarding school in 1930. The two of
them lived mainly on the top floor of the house in Mallord Street, in the adjoining day and night nurseries.

Christopher said: 'So much were we together that Nanny became almost a part of me ... Other people hovered round the edges, but they meant little. My total loyalty was to her.' He said his father's picture of her in 'Buckingham Palace' was entirely inaccurate. She was not the sort of person who would brush off a child's question with a meaningless 'Sure to, dear, but it's time for tea'. And writing of 'Disobedience', the 'James James Morrison Morrison' poem, Christopher Milne maintained that, although he could not be sure how he felt about anything at the age of three, 'I can only guess that, though I might not have missed my mother, and would certainly not have missed my father, I would have missed Nanny – most desolately.'

Olive Rand was no ordinary nanny; she had had a far more challenging experience than most. She had been nanny to the Chilean ambassador's children in London and had travelled widely with them. Indeed, in 1914 they had been stranded in France for a while at the beginning of the war and she had then gone with them to America and Chile. She spoke to the *Sunday Times* about A. A. Milne in 1965, with the air of one who had been asked the questions many times before but was still not tired of the subject: 'He never scorned Christopher Robin's fancies and if the boy wanted his nursery pets to be included in conversations and games, Mr Milne always entered into the spirit of the thing and spoke to the toys as if they were real people.' Olive Rand had a fiancé who worked as a Post Office engineer after his discharge from the Army and who kept hoping Olive would leave Christopher and get married, but she could not bring herself to leave the child until he no longer had need of her.

By the summer of 1921 A. A. Milne had finished two plays, *The Truth about Blayds* and *The Dover Road*, which were to become, like *Mr Pim Passes By*, not only successes in London and New York, but staples of amateur dramatic societies and repertory companies all over the world. The success of his plays in that heyday of amateur dramatics was such that he could tell John Drinkwater in 1924 that he was making £2,000 a year from amateur rights alone. 'He is going ahead at a tremendous rate,' his father said on 6 June. If one wonders what he did with the rather staggering results of his popular success, it is obvious that he realised, like any writer, that it could not last. He lived well – but most of his money he invested against an uncertain future.

On 26 June, J. V. Milne wrote again and told his friend that the child's aunt reported Billy to be adorable, which suggests that his grandparents had not been seeing much of him, if indeed they had seen him at all. In June, Alan promised to motor down in August, but it was September before they got there, though it was hardly a difficult journey. Billy was thirteen months old. 'So his grandmother saw him to her great happiness.' She was already 'deaf, too blind to read or work, and not able to cross the room without a stick.' She died not long afterwards.

It is not unreasonable to imagine that the child's teddy bear (a present from Harrods on his first birthday the month before) made the journey to Burgess Hill too, in September 1921. He was not yet called Winnie-the-Pooh, but he was already a palpable presence in the household as Christopher Robin tried out his first words. He managed an impressive 'Owdyerdo' at eighteen months, when his father said he was 'in tremendous form now, just walking and talking and trying to do both without stopping all day'. His bear was simply Bear or Teddy or more grandly, to his elders, Edward Bear. 'A row of teddy-bears sitting in a toy-shop, all one size, all one price. Yet how different each is from the next. Some look stand-offish, some look loveable. And one in particular, the one over there, has a specially endearing expression. Yes, that's the one we would like, please.' So Christopher Milne in his autobiography, imagining the purchasing of Winnie-the-Pooh. What he does not admit is that the bear we know, the bear who would become familiar to millions from E. H. Shepard's drawings, is not really his bear at all, but another bear from an earlier nursery, of quite different shape and already with a pronounced character of his own: Graham Shepard's Growler.

Growler was, according to Shepard, 'a magnificent bear. I have never seen his like.' In 1915, when Shepard had been at home and the family away, he had written to his son, seven-year-old Graham: 'Growler and Puck have been an awful nuisance; they talk and jabber all night.' Puck was a mere 'cork-filled gnome' and not part of our story, but it is obvious that Growler was a real character and would play an important part in the forming of our image of Winnie-the-Pooh.

In the same month, September 1921, the Milne family paid the first of several visits to a thatched cottage called the Decoy at Poling, near Arundel and Littlehampton in Sussex. It was at the Decoy that Christopher Robin fed the swan on the lake and called him Pooh. 'This is a very fine name for a swan, because if you call him and he doesn't come (which is a thing swans are good at), then you can pretend that you were just saying "Pooh!" to show how little you wanted him.' There were cows who came down to drink at this lake and Milne couldn't help thinking: 'Moo rhymes with Pooh! Surely there is a bit of poetry to be got out of that . . .' And there would eventually be one poem with a swan and another with cows, but with neither a Moo nor a Pooh in either of them, because that is the way it often happens with poems.

In July 1922, they stayed for a month with a Mrs Hobbs in Woolacombe Bay in Devon. This was the place, Christopher says, where he first encountered 'sand-between-the-toes', though, at not yet two, he was still at the age for eating it and really too small for clutching sixpences tight. (A more likely venue for that poem would be Whitesand Bay near Plas Brondanw in Wales, where they were the following summer, when the poem was written.) Swinnerton wrote to Woolacombe: 'If the weather where you are has been anything like the weather I have been having on Arnold Bennett's yacht, I am sorry for you. On the other hand, if it has kept you indoors to write more plays, it has done good work, and in that case only Billy and his mother are to be sympathised with.' Milne replied to 'beloved Swin': 'We've had three fine days and spend most of our time changing our clothes. But we enjoy ourselves and Billy and Daff are blooming. So am I. And also very slack. When I return to London, I shall WORK; a constant stream of GREAT PLAYS and POWERFUL NOVELS will flow from my pen.'

Writing to Swinnerton, Milne was always at his most self-mockingly boastful.

The Milnes would soon be looking for a country place of their own. Kenneth Grahame offered Boham's at Blewbury in Berkshire, which he was leaving in the anguished aftermath of his son's death on the Oxford railway line. But Milne wanted to buy, not rent, and in the meantime the Decoy would do.

Milne had been in contact with Grahame because of Curtis Brown's suggestion that he should dramatise *The Wind in the Willows*. The play was not produced until 1929 – after Milne's own success with his children's books – but it was as early as 1921 that Milne responded to his agent's suggestion. Curtis Brown had been trying to get managements interested in it earlier, but had reactions to the idea very much like that of the publishers themselves when the book was first written. When they finally accepted it, Methuen had not even had enough faith in the book to pay a guaranteed advance. But in spite of the famous *Times Literary Supplement* review ('As a contribution to natural history, the work is negligible') and Arthur Ransome's in the *Bookman* ('If we judge the book by its aim, it is a failure, like a speech to Hottentots made in Chinese'), it is difficult to believe, from the list of editions that followed, that *The Wind in the Willows* was as much in need of Milne's one-man crusade to publicise it as he always suggested. Already in 1921, thirteen years after its first publication, it had gone into eleven editions. Milne was always pressing it on his friends. In 1919 he wrote of *The Wind in the Willows* as 'a book which should be a classic, but is not'.

Usually I speak about it at my first meeting with a stranger. It is my opening remark, just as yours is something futile about the weather. If I don't get it in at the beginning, I squeeze it in at the end. The stranger has got to have it some time. Should I ever find myself in the dock, and one never knows, my answer to the question whether I had anything to say, would be, 'Well, my lord, if I might just recommend a book to the jury before leaving . . .'

and much later, in an introduction to a new edition, Milne added:

One does not argue about *The Wind in the Willows*. The young man gives it to the girl with whom he is in love, and if she does not like it, asks her to return his letters. The older man tries it on his nephew, and alters his will accordingly. The book is a test of character . . . When you sit down to it, don't be so ridiculous as to suppose that you are sitting in judgment on my taste, or on the art of Kenneth Grahame. You are merely sitting in judgment on yourself.

Some people would come to feel the same way about *Winnie-the-Pooh*. There is no doubt at all, though the links are subtle, that *The Wind in the Willows* lies behind *Winnie-the-Pooh* and that, without it, Milne's book might well not have been written. Milne, like Grahame, remembered his childhood as the great, good time. 'The queer thing is,' said Grahame, 'I can remember everything I felt then. The part of my brain I used from four till seven can never have altered.' Coming back to the Thames Valley wakened every recollection for Grahame. Milne had no such clearly defined childhood playground to return to, but it was all there inside his head. E. H. Shepard would report that one of the first questions Milne asked him was indeed whether he had read *The Wind in the Willows*. This was long before he illustrated it (not until 1931) and made the link between Grahame and Milne seem ever closer. 'I realised even then,' Shepard said, 'what a very great influence it had been on him. It all seemed to come from that, and he was quite frank about it. He was an honest bloke; he had an admiration for the book.' No wonder that when Curtis Brown wrote to him with the proposal that he should dramatise it, Milne responded like this on 15 November 1921:

> The Wind in the Willows – *now you're talking!*
> *If Kenneth Grahame is willing, and if you feel*
> *pretty sure that you can find the right manager for*
> *it (as I think you should be able to), I will do it.*
> *And I shall love doing it. In fact, as soon as I got*
> *your letter, I began sketching it out, and I think I*
> *see how it can be done. I think it should be a*
> *children's play, with a little incidental music.*

*   *   *

Alan Milne would tell his brother Ken that he had become 'sick of and entirely uninterested in politics' since the war. That was certainly true of party politics but he continued to hold his strong pacifist convictions and to follow the international news closely, reading both *The Times* and the more left-wing *Daily News* at this period. As a pacifist who had experienced the Somme, Milne was even more deeply concerned than most that that should indeed have been the war to end all wars. It was bitter to realise already how unlikely that was to be so. In September 1922, Lloyd George nearly brought the country to war with Turkey. It was when, having encouraged the Greeks to invade Turkey (after the nationalist revolt which threatened to upset the allied post-war settlement), Lloyd George saw the Turks rout the Greeks and move right up to the barbed wire of the British positions at Chanak in the Neutral Zone. There was not only a threat to navigation in the Straits but, some said, a debt owed to the British war dead at Gallipoli. This chauvinistic suggestion was ridiculed by A. A. Milne in the *Daily News* on 4 October 1922 in an article which impressed E. M. Forster:

> They have almost brought it off, the War to End Peace, for which they have been striving for three years. What an incredible joke! A war 'to defend the freedom of the Straits and the sanctity of our graves in Gallipoli', says *Punch* magnificently. Of course you can think of it like that, and it sounds quite dignified and natural. But you may also think, as I do, of those five or ten or twenty men, our chosen statesmen, sitting round a table; the same old statesmen; each with his war memories thick upon him; each knowing his own utter incompetence to maintain a war or to end a war ...

Forster, taking up Milne's title, 'Another Little War', wrote five days later:

> Sir, – Mr A. A. Milne's brilliant article deserves special thanks for its scathing analysis of 'the sanctity of our graves in Gallipoli'. Our rulers knew that their policy would not be popular, and in the hope of stampeding us into it they permitted this vile appeal – the viler because the sentiment that it tries to pervert is a noble one and purifies the life of a nation when directed rightly. The bodies of the young men who are buried out there have no quarrel with one another now, no part in our quarrels or interest in our patronage, no craving for holocausts of more young men. Anyone who has himself entered, however feebly, into the life of the spirit, can realise this.
>
> It is only the elderly ghouls of Whitehall who exhume the dead for the purpose of party propaganda and employ them as a bait to catch the living.

Forster and Milne never met, but this warm support from the distinguished writer must have returned to Milne's mind two years later when *A Passage to India* was published. It is tempting to imagine that he might have felt he could really have written a powerful novel himself, if only he had had some wider experiences, if only he had been a different person.

Christopher Milne said that there were really very few things his parents enjoyed doing together. They had been married for ten years and certainly Alan had given up hope that Daphne would become a golfer. She had had lessons but she had never really taken to it. Harvey Nichols and Harrods were the playgrounds she preferred. What she enjoyed most of all was something Alan hated – having the decorators in and changing the appearance of a room. Alan would retreat to his study – a small dark room at the back of the house – and try to ignore the upheaval and the smell of paint. He would make all the right appreciative noises when it was safe to come out again. Daphne spent a great deal of time at her hairdresser's and at Elizabeth Arden being groomed. She was not in the least beautiful but she was beautifully turned out – immaculate and untouchable. People described her as glamorous, sophisticated and elegant. She enjoyed her dressmaker and visiting her milliner; her clothes and hats were very important to her.

She wore a particularly splendid hat to the dress rehearsal of one of Milne's plays. One hopes there was no one sitting behind her. Milne told Irene Vanbrugh a story that suggests how different they were. Apparently, the dress designer, 'Madame Handeley Seymour' of New Bond Street – who had been responsible for the leading lady's clothes – told Milne that she had never seen a more lovely hat than the one his wife was wearing. Daphne was thrilled. She felt, Milne said, 'as I would feel if Thomas Hardy patted me on the head'. There was very little chance of that happening. Though Hardy lived for another four-and-a-half years, he and Milne never met. Barrie could easily have arranged a meeting, but he must have realised that Hardy would have no interest in Milne, however much interest Milne had in Hardy. 'How I loathe Christopher Robin,' Florence Hardy would one day say, perhaps with a touch of sour grapes as her own children's stories had had so little success.

There had been a long, admiring article in the *Boston Transcript* two years earlier by J. Brooks Atkinson, which urged Milne not to 'stoop to pot-boilers and routine pieces of hack-work. Mr Milne's knowledge of human nature and his bubbling sense of humor qualify him for more note-worthy achievement.' Certainly, he didn't want to write pot-boilers and he had no need to. He regretted having signed a contract with Curtis Brown on 15 November 1922 for three novels: the first was supposed to be published in 1923, following *The Red House Mystery*. An American editor had been so impressed by that novel that on his next trip to London he made his own contract with Milne, offering him no less than £2,000 for the serial rights of his next mystery story. But there never was another one. And his next novel did not appear until 1931. Perhaps it was his admiration for Jane Austen, for Samuel Butler, for Thomas Hardy, that made the novel so difficult for him. He was not sure he could write the sort of novel he would want to read.

There would be other plays, but now it seemed time for a change. During the previous winter, Milne had written a poem for Daphne (it was not a children's poem) inspired by a glimpse of Billy, aged two, kneeling by his cot, being taught by his nanny to say the words so many children have been taught to say: 'God bless Mummy, Daddy and Nanny and make me a good boy.' 'Mr Milne crept in and watched for a few moments,' Olive Brockwell (as the nanny became) remembered many years later. 'Then I heard him going away down the stairs chuckling as if he was very pleased about something.' With hindsight she thought A. A. Milne was 'chuckling' because he had come up with a brilliant idea for a poem. 'Such lovely words,' she said. 'And they were true. I did have a dressing gown hanging on the door of the nursery.' But Milne was surely smiling first, of course, because the child looked so sweet and, secondly, because he seemed so perfectly to embody the fact that prayer meant nothing at all to a small boy. Indeed, it meant very little to Milne himself. Milne had no time at all for orthodox Christianity.

The sight of a child at prayer 'is one over which thousands have been sentimental,' Milne wrote in his autobiography. 'It is indeed calculated to bring a lump to the throat. But, even so, one must tell the truth about the matter.' And the truth is not only that prayer means nothing to a two-year-old but that, although children do have 'an artless beauty, an innocent grace', along with 'this outstanding physical quality, there is a natural lack of moral quality, which expresses itself, as Nature always insists on expressing herself, in an egotism entirely ruthless.'

The critic Humphrey Carpenter pointed out that there was really no need for 'Beachcomber' to parody the poem, not long after it first appeared. ('Hush, hush, nobody cares! / Christopher Robin has fallen downstairs.') 'Vespers' itself is intended to be an entirely ironic picture of childhood. It is interesting that in his memoir of his childhood, Christopher Milne himself disputes what he calls his father's 'cynical' attitude. A. A. Milne was obviously putting it forward so strongly to counteract the general idea of 'Vespers' as a sentimental poem about a good little boy saying his prayers. But his son himself felt much closer to Wordsworth's view of childhood than his father's. He remembered 'those first affections, those shadowy recollections' as 'the fountain light of all our day'. Adults, though better at disguising it, are often as heartlessly egotistic as children.

> In those days of splendour and glory I certainly felt myself nearer to God – the God that Nanny was telling me about, who lived up in the sky – than I do today. And so, asked to choose between those two views of childhood, I'm bound to say that I'm for Wordsworth. Maybe he is just being sentimental. Maybe the infant William has fooled the middle-aged poet in the same way that the kneeling Christopher Robin fooled so many of his readers. Maybe my cynical father is right. But this is not how I feel about it.

Alan Milne gave the poem 'Vespers' to Daphne as a present. He told her that if she liked to get it published she could keep the money. She sent it to *Vanity Fair* in New York. It appeared in January 1923 and she received $50. Over the years, 'Vespers' proved the most lavish present Milne had ever given his wife. (One remembers that

Walter de la Mare is supposed to have sent a son through Eton on the proceeds of 'The Listeners'.) The following winter Milne would be invited to provide one of the tiny books in the library of Lutyens's elaborate Queen's Dolls' House, which was to be shown at the Empire Exhibition at Wembley before finding a permanent home at Windsor. The whole scheme was 'ineradicably silly', Arthur Benson suggested, but it was in the nature of a royal command. It seems only George Bernard Shaw refused and 'in a very rude manner', according to Princess Marie Louise; Milne dutifully copied out 'Vespers'. At least it was short. For many years afterwards there would be copies of 'Vespers' hanging in nurseries all over the world, with the words at the bottom: 'Reprinted by permission from the Library of the Queen's Dolls' House'. Milne was already, though he did not yet know it, on his way to becoming some sort of poet laureate of the nursery.

3

WHEN WE WERE
VERY YOUNG

There was a house party in north Wales in the summer of 1923. Milne had agreed to share with Nigel Playfair the cost of the lease of a house belonging to Clough Williams-Ellis, who would soon develop Portmeirion nearby. It was Plas Brondanw at Llanfrothen near Portmadoc. It is in a peculiarly beautiful part of Britain. The Londoners looked forward to walking up Cnicht and Snowdon, to exploring Harlech Castle and to bathing in Cardigan Bay.

Playfair was feeling rich and generous as a result of his production of *The Beggar's Opera* and issued lots of invitations. Frederic Austin, who had adapted the music for Gay's entertainment, was there, and Grace Lovat Fraser, the wife of the designer, and Joan Pitt-Chapman, aged sixteen, whose father had played Macheath but had died during the run. There was also a woman called Mrs Malcolm, whose husband had recently been accused and acquitted of murder. There were others, too, coming and going. The novelist Richard Hughes and his mother came to supper one evening and found themselves warmly welcomed by Mrs Playfair – 'Oh do come in, Mrs Beard and Mr Beard.' It was the way the family were accustomed to refer to them, for no better reason than that Richard Hughes had a beard at that time. The rest of the evening was a little sticky. Everyone had heard the welcome.

It was a strange house party. All might have been well if the weather had been good and the planned expeditions had been able to take place. But 'it rains all day in Wales', Milne wrote gloomily to Swinnerton. All day and almost every day. Giles Playfair, aged thirteen, took some photographs with his Kodak Brownie on one of the three fine days and glowered at the assembled company. 'I disliked everyone who neglected to take the trouble to interest themselves in me. Very few people did. Certainly the house-party in Wales (the Milnes included) found me a silent, sulky, dull and stupid boy.' His brother Lyon shone in comparison, writing a play about Perkin Warbeck and reading it aloud one wet afternoon to his audience's amusement. Milne sat down there and then to write a preface.

Nigel Playfair made tremendous efforts to keep everyone's spirits up as wet day followed wet day. He was determined people should enjoy themselves. His son Giles remembered:

While he was about, everyone was laughing despite their depression at the persistent climatic gloom. He always came down last to breakfast. Before he arrived, no noise emerged from the dining room save the desultory clatter of knife and fork on plate. But his entry was invariably a signal for an outburst of wild merriment which continued unabated until the meal was finished.

He made us all play an absurd game called 'I met a sheep'. The rules of this game were simple. You said to your next-door neighbour 'I met a sheep', who replied, 'What did it do?' You then waved both hands and explained, 'It went, "ba, ba, ba".' The game continued until everyone round the table was intoning, 'ba, ba, ba' and waving both hands. The sight of young and old, diffident and superior, famous and obscure, all indulging in this curious ritual was irresistible.

The game, in fact, did little to dispel Milne's gloom. Moreover, there was a depressing butler called Griffiths (who had come with the house), who seemed to have taken a particular dislike to Milne, always serving him last, when the food was lukewarm. And Billy, aged three that month, had been whisked away to the nursery wing with his nanny to join the youngest Playfair, four-year-old Andrew, and was rarely seen. Indeed, Joan, the then sixteen-year-old, looking back, could not even remember the infant, absorbed as she was in her grief at the death of her father and trying to concentrate on a black-and-white check dress she was making – but she did remember Alan and Daphne Milne. In her memory, the holiday seemed a sort of background 'out of which that couple protruded'. She was particularly interested in A. A. Milne because she had had a small part as one of the children in his play *Make-Believe* at Hammersmith, five years earlier. She had never met Daphne before, and now she found them, ten years married, 'honey-mooney, as they were always together and speaking very little to anyone else'. She thought them 'a nice and attractive couple, both tall and he ascetic-looking and serious, not laughy', as one might have expected.

Giles Playfair confirmed her memory, saying, 'They adored each other.' He found Milne himself 'prudish, very, very proper', disliking anything vulgar. 'Oh, yes,' he said, 'my father and he liked each other very much.' But obviously, to the thirteen-year-old, the well-known playwright was not at all as he felt a writer should be. When one lists the things Milne disliked one can easily see how priggish he could have appeared to young Giles Playfair. He disliked not only beer, but gin and whisky too. ('Why are you the devil of a fellow if you like drinking whisky, and the devil of a prig if you don't?' as a boy in one of Milne's plays would ask.) He disliked professional football and hated all blood sports ('the taste for killing small animals'). He had no interest in racing and disliked all gambling – the whole business of getting something for nothing, whether the gambling was on sport, on the stock exchange or on a state lottery (the possibility of one was being discussed at this time). Milne had no time for jazz; he was not particularly interested, in fact, in any kind of music – though he once enjoyed a cello recital, by one of his cousins, rather more than he expected. Above all, Milne loathed, and made clear that he loathed, all forms of aggression, all unthinking talk of the glories of war. It was rather a rebarbative collection of feelings for a thirteen-year-old to stomach.

Milne became increasingly irritated by the proximity of his fellow guests. 'In a week,' he wrote later, 'I was screaming with agoraphobia' – not claustrophobia, but the dislike of public places, dislike of the drawing-room.

He needed to get away. The post one day brought him, forwarded from Chelsea, the proof of a poem he had written for Rose Fyleman for a new children's magazine she was starting, called *The Merry-Go-Round*. Milne retreated gladly to a summer house to correct the proof.

Rose Fyleman was the author of numerous books for children, with such titles as *Fairies and Chimneys* and *The Fairy Flute*. Fairies were fashionable in the early 1920s. Children, if not just an attractive form of interior decoration, were seen as imaginative little creatures whose fancies must be allowed to flourish and not be quashed by sceptical adults. There was some feeling that children should be sealed off in pretty nurseries from the painful realities of the outside world and there was a tremendous suspicion of 'progressive' parents who, like some of their Victorian predecessors, but for very different reasons, distrusted fairy tales and those who offered sails to minds that rather required ballast. Compton Mackenzie would satirise parents who surrounded their children with nothing but Meccano and clever mechanical toys and who offered them *The Wonder Book of Why and What*, concentrating on pictures of steam engines and aeroplanes, and banning 'stupid stories about fairies, or ghosts, or the heroes of the past'. There was a revulsion from their tendency to explain that the rings in the grass are actually caused by fungi or that Cinderella's glass slipper, through an error in translation, was actually made of fur.

Rose Fyleman was also editing the annual *Joy Street*, which was published for the first time that year, just a month after the first issue of *Merry-Go-Round*. *Joy Street* was promoted as 'a meeting place for literally all the best writing for children', but Rose Fyleman was definitely on the side of the fairies. Her famous, banal 'There are fairies at the bottom of our garden!' was only one of scores of verses she contributed to *Punch* in the 1920s, verses that were certainly not intended to be funny. It was only a year since Arthur Conan Doyle in *The Coming of the Fairies* had examined the case of the Cottingley fairies, those much-publicised photographs which seem such obvious fakes, and yet on which he returned an open verdict.

'It is too late for a modern mother,' Milne wrote in 1925, 'to wonder if her children ought to be brought up with a belief in fairies. Their acceptance of fairies is as natural as their acceptance of the Milkman or the Mayor . . . To say that a child has no need for fairies when there are so many beautiful birds and butterflies in the world, or no need for seven-league boots so long as five and five most wonderfully make ten, is like saying that a man has no need for Switzerland until he has exhausted (as none of us has) England, nor any need for Wordsworth until he has mastered every line of Shakespeare.'

The trouble was that most fairy stories and poems were feeble by any standard. Enid Blyton's second book was published this year. It was called *Real Fairies*, and the *Morning Post* commented, 'Children have received a new educational charter restoring their right to believe in fairies.' The *Morning Post* had obviously forgotten the children's answer to Peter Pan's regular question each Christmas, saving the dying Tinkerbell.

In 1924 there was also, nauseatingly, *The 'Normous Saturday Fairy Book*, which included some verses by Marion St John Webb, the author of *The Littlest One*, which had first appeared in 1914 and had sold 50,000 copies by this time. It was a collection of verses told in the first person by a six-year-old boy, complete with lisp and appropriate spelling. Milne had himself, years earlier, poured scorn on the taste for baby-talk. 'It is important,' one of his characters had said long ago, 'that even as a child he should always be addressed in rational English and not in that ridiculous baby-talk so common to young mothers', and had then been challenged himself for calling the child 'his nunkey's ickle petsy wetsy lambkin'. There was masses of it in *Punch* – but also some signs of a revulsion against it, as in an A. E. Bestall cartoon in which a nurse says to her charge: 'Look, Dickie, what a dear little bow wow!' and the child replies coolly: 'Do you mean the Cairn or the Sealyham?' People often found it quite hard not to use such talk, to address a tiny child as straightforwardly as someone of their own size. And in rendering children's own speech, many writers (even H. G. Wells) apparently did not blush to write 'pritty f'owers' or 'Do it adain, Dadda'. Milne actually used the device sparingly, but would come to regret using it at all when Dorothy Parker got hold of him.

The poem, whose proof he was correcting in that Welsh summer house as the rain poured down, was the first he had written deliberately for children, but there were no children in it, no baby talk and no fairies. When Rose Fyleman first approached him, he had said no. In 1925, two years later, he said it was on the grounds that he was too busy, but that then he began to wonder what he would have written if he hadn't been too busy. In 1939, in his autobiography, when he was so intent on denying the label of children's writer, he gave a slightly different explanation. He said he told her he didn't write verse for children: 'I didn't and couldn't, it wasn't in my line.' And then, after he had posted his letter turning down the suggestion, he began to wonder what he might have written if he had not refused; and then he did write it, and it turned out to be one of the best of all Milne's children's poems – 'The Dormouse and the Doctor'. The misguided doctor in the original illustrations by Harry Rowntree is himself a rather large rodent, in top hat and striped trousers, prescribing milk and massage-of-the-back, and freedom-from-worry and drives-in-a-car, and above all chrysanthemums, quite oblivious of the fact that there is nothing at all wrong with the dormouse, except for a longing

> *to be back in a bed*
> *Of delphiniums (blue) and geraniums (red).*

There was a lot wrong with poetry for children in 1923, quite apart from the prevalence of fairies. Viscountess Grey of Falloden, in her introduction to *A Child's Book of Lyrics*, compiled by Philip Wayne and published by Methuen that year, wrote of the time as being 'this age of psycho-analysis when everyone is becoming aware of the importance of first impressions'. And yet, she went on, 'If I could buy up all the Christmas annuals and school periodicals and magazines that provide verse written specially for children and burn these things publicly in the marketplace, I would do it with both hands. The mass of sickly nonsense of this nature that appears today is a great evil. Popular carelessness allows rubbish to be given to children for no better reason than that children are

young.' 'They don't get any richness into their words –
they don't get any flavour. There's no bite', as Milne put it
in a story about a poet's daughter. (This poet's first poem
about his child, had, owing to a misunderstanding, been
used to wedge the nursery window, which rattled at night.
It was probably the fate the poem deserved.)

When Milne had finished correcting his proof, the
work of only a few minutes, and had addressed the envelope to Rose Fyleman, he had to think of an excuse not
to return to the house and his fellow guests. Obviously, he
must write something. One might think of him, standing,
looking out of the summer-house window at the relentless
Welsh downpour and trying to cheer himself up.

> Is it raining? *Never mind—*
> *Think how much the birdies love it!*
> *See them in their dozens drawn,*
> *Dancing, to the croquet lawn—*
> *Could our little friends have dined*
> *If there'd been no worms above it?*
> Is it murky? *What of that,*
> *If the owls are fairly perky?*
> *Just imagine you were one—*
> *Wouldn't you* detest *the sun?*

Milne had written that a couple of years earlier: not as a children's poem, of course, but just for fun, on another wet summer's day. Perhaps writing children's poems wasn't so much out of his line after all. And he certainly wasn't too busy. He sat down and started playing with words. He had a reddish marbled quarto exercise book and a pencil with an eraser on it ('just the thing for poetry'). He felt slightly embarrassed about what he was doing, as so many children's writers have done over the years. Wouldn't it sound much better if he could report progress each evening at dinner on that second detective story everyone was so keen for him to write? (He could not help remembering he had been offered a contract for £2,000 for the serial rights alone.) It was, perhaps, all right to be turning out some children's verses on holiday – but was it really what he wanted his next book to be? Writing for children was not taken very seriously. It was something, people thought, that anyone might do in an idle moment. But Milne never underestimated the genre. He remembered *The Wind in the Willows*, the book he had admired for so long, and knew that 'no one can write a book which children will like, unless he writes it for himself first.'

That the book, when written, should satisfy children must be regarded as a happy accident, just as one regards it as a happy accident if a dog or a child loves one; it is a matter of personality, and personality is the last matter about which one can take thought. But whatever fears one has, one need not fear that one is writing too well for a child . . . It is difficult enough to express oneself with all the words in the dictionary at one's disposal. With none but simple words, the difficulty is much greater. We need not spare ourselves.

Not that Milne believed in a strictly limited vocabulary; he wanted his words to have richness, flavour and bite, and he knew the power of the occasional unfamiliar word – just as Beatrix Potter did when she commented in *The Flopsy Bunnies* on the report that the effect of eating too much lettuce is 'soporific'. If one hears a small child refer to someone as 'well-intentioned' ('Ernest was an elephant and very well-intentioned') or to someone else 'wandering vaguely quite of her own accord', one knows one is in the presence of a Milne-listener. But most of the language in A. A. Milne's children's poems is, without being boring to an adult, easily understood by a three- or four-year-old, and that is a remarkable achievement. Milne wanted to make his position quite clear. He said of his first collection that it 'is not the work of a poet becoming playful, nor of a lover of children expressing his love, nor of a prose-writer knocking together a few jingles for the little ones, it is the work of a light-verse writer taking his job seriously, even though he is taking it into the nursery.' Milne's technical skill is admirable. It is his dextrous use of rhythm and rhyme that makes his children's poems lodge in the head, and this was what he most wanted. He said once in a preface addressed to young readers:

Now you know of course that verses have rhymes in them; but even more important than the rhymes is what is called 'rhythm'. It is a difficult-looking word, but what it means is just 'the time that the verse keeps'. Every piece of poetry has a music of its own which it is humming to itself as it goes along, and every line, every word, in it has to keep time to this music. This is what makes it difficult to write poetry; because you can't use any words in any order as long as it's sense and grammar, but you have to use particular words in a particular order, so that they keep time to the music, and rhyme when you want them to. If you can find words which keep time to the music, and which are just the words you want to say, then the verses which you write are verses which sing themselves into people's heads, and stay there for ever, so that even when they are alone and unhappy they have this music with them for company.

Milne also made it clear that there were three sources for the poems. 'There are three ways in which a writer knows about people: by remembering, by noticing, and by imagining.' He was remembering his own childhood, the things he and his brother Ken had done, the things he had felt himself. 'As a child I kept a mouse; probably it escaped – they generally do. Christopher Robin has kept almost everything except a mouse. But he did go to Buckingham Palace a good deal (which I didn't) . . . And most children hop . . . and sometimes they sit halfway down the stairs.' He was obviously 'noticing' his small son, never very far from his thoughts. Billy had a new pair of braces and was proud of them. Perhaps they were a present for that third birthday in Wales. Certainly 'Growing Up' was one of the poems that was written in the summer house and so was 'Happiness', as the small boy splashed through the puddles in his Great Big Waterproof Boots. In that poem Milne called the child John (as he had often called Ken in his writing). Although Christopher Robin comes 'very trippingly off the tongue', as Milne remarked, it certainly didn't work in that poem. In fact, as Milne said, 'Christopher Robin is definitely associated with only three sets of verses'. He is actually named in four out of forty-four in that first collection. But even Milne, for all his remembering and observing, could not resist imagining a few fairies, though Twinkletoes (without the illustration) could easily be a butterfly.

Milne had written about a quarter of the book by the time they left Wales. Giles Playfair suggests the Milnes left early:

> They decided to cut their holiday short and leave before the proper time. They were at no pains to conceal their pleasure at going and I shall never forget their happiness on the morning of departure.
>
> My father, however, refused to be outdone. He made his family and house-party see the Milnes off. We were instructed to form a circle round their car and sing in lusty voices, 'The Milnes are going, hurray, hurray,' to the tune of 'The Campbells are coming . . .' The Milnes drove away with the song ringing in their ears.

Milne now had to break the news to his agent and publishers that his next book was to be not the detective story or straight novel they were hoping for, but a collection of children's verse. John Macrae of Dutton's was over in London that autumn. He had published both *The Red*

House Mystery and a collection of *Punch* pieces, *The Sunny Side*, in New York the year before. Milne took him to lunch at the Garrick. There was talk of Milne making his first visit to America in the winter. 'So far it is mostly talk. But I have promised to so often that I must. We feel it would be good for trade.' It would be another eight years before he got there. His American publisher remembered:

> During the halting conversation, which is likely to take place between author and publisher, Mr Milne genially informed me that he was about to send me his new manuscript – a volume of poetry for children. We are all aware that probably the most hopeless kind of manuscript a publisher expects to receive from his favourite author is that of poetry for children.
>
> I have no complaint about children's poetry by a genius. However, Milne had not yet demonstrated that he could write poetry. You can imagine my chagrin and disappointment. However, I covered up my feelings and held them in harness until the manuscript arrived.

Milne was aware of Macrae's lack of enthusiasm for the project and he realised himself, as he indicated in a letter to Irene Vanbrugh in late September, what a mixed collection the poems were.

I am writing a book of children's verses. Like Stevenson, only better. No, not a bit like Stevenson really. More like Milne. But they are a curious collection; some for children, some about children, some by, with or from children.

In this same letter, we get a glimpse of the daily life of father and son. They went for a walk after breakfast every morning in their indoor shoes and without hats ('quite informal, not party at all'). They walked each day as far as the Fulham Road and then home again by a different route. Every day they passed the same middle-aged postman. One day Milne said, 'Say good morning to the postman.' Three-year-old Billy obediently said, 'Good morning.' When the postman took no notice whatsoever, the child sensibly suggested, 'He doesn't know me', which seemed to his father 'a dignified way of concluding the episode'. Only too soon a great many people would know the child and murmurs of 'That's Christopher Robin!' would accompany his walks.

In October, E. V. Lucas seems to have been worried that Milne was playing too much golf. He thought Milne would be the better for a little more structure in his life and suggested that he should start writing regular prose again for *Punch*. Milne did not resent Lucas's advice about his 'literary career'. 'I have always been grateful to you for your interest in it', but he rejected the suggestion that he was idle – though he hesitated to mention that, for the moment, he really had no need to work, with money constantly flowing in from performances of the plays all over the place. A production of *The Truth about Blayds* by Liverpool Rep had been a particular success and earned Milne the best review (in the *Manchester Guardian* from C. E. Montague) that he said he had ever had in his life. *Mr Pim Passes By* even ran for three months in Berlin in a German translation and accumulated 'a trifle of two thousand billion marks or so' at that time of runaway inflation in Germany. *Mr Pim* was also put on in Vienna that year. Milne wrote to Lucas:

> *I think my indolence is more apparent than real; or perhaps I should say that it is real, but I overcome it pretty well. I have written in the last five years: six full-length plays, four short plays, two novels, about a book and a half of essays and sketches, a book of verses, three short stories and various oddments: in addition, of course, to the more mechanical labour of seeing 9 books through the press, and rehearsing seven full-length plays, which is not too bad.*

*Quite frankly I could not bear to write regularly
for* Punch *again. I'm sorry, but there it is. It
would make me miserable. And I suspect that what
you really want is that 'Billy Book' you have been
urging me to write; and you feel that, if I began a
few chapters for* Punch, *I should be more likely to
pull it off. Fear not. I will do it yet. I like writing;
the sort of writing which doesn't come into plays;
and I will do that book, or some other book,
directly, which will make you say 'I always said he
could write.'*

*I will send you 20 or 30 of the poems next week,
if you would like to see them – officially as
Methuen's friend, or unofficially as mine. A mixed
lot. So mixed that I think (hooray!) that they will
require a prose introduction.*

The poems duly arrived in Lucas's office at Methuen.
E. V. Lucas was extremely influential at both Methuen
and *Punch* at this time. He was just about to become
chairman of Methuen and he had been the editor Owen
Seaman's deputy at *Punch* from the days when Milne had
first worked there. Although in his memoir *Reading,
Writing and Remembering* Lucas praises both Milne and
'his collaborator with the pencil, Ernest Shepard', he does

not himself claim responsibility for that remarkable partnership, which was to seem as apt and inevitable as
Gilbert and Sullivan. But there seems no question that it
was his idea.

As soon as Lucas saw the children's poems, he realised
that they would make a splendid book when there were
enough of them, and that, in the meantime, some of them
should appear in *Punch*. It was obviously important to
find the right illustrator. 'Vespers' had not been illustrated
when it first appeared and Harry Rowntree, who drew
the pictures for 'The Dormouse and the Doctor', was
extremely good at animals (he spent days at the London
Zoo), but not so much at home in the nursery. Lucas
was sitting next to Shepard at the *Punch* Table, a sociable editorial meeting, when he suggested (so Shepard
remembered) doing some drawings and seeing what
Milne thought of them.

Milne knew Shepard's work well, though Shepard had
not actually joined the Table until 1921, after Milne had
left *Punch*. Before the war, when Shepard was contributing his first cartoons, Milne had actually said more than
once to the art editor, F. H. Townsend, 'What on earth
do you see in this man? He's perfectly hopeless.' And
Townsend had replied complacently, 'You wait.' Shepard
had always had difficulty with the jokes.

The Shepard who illustrated Milne's first collection of children's poems, and who would go on to illustrate the other children's books, was the one for whom Milne had waited. As men, they had very little in common – despite some odd links. For instance, there was the fact that they had lived as small children only a few streets apart, and Shepard had actually been at the same kindergarten in Upper Baker Street as Milne's friend Nigel Playfair. Later, Shepard's sister Ethel had been bridesmaid at the wedding of John Vine Milne's most famous ex-pupil, Alfred Harmsworth, later Lord Northcliffe and eventually owner of *The Times*. Harmsworth, who had showered pennies on small Alan Milne, had taught young Ernest Shepard how to bowl overarm. That was not much of a basis for friendship, and they were of very different temperament. Milne found Shepard's attitude to the war particularly hard to take. They had both experienced the horror of the Somme in 1916 – and Shepard had gone on to win the Military Cross at Passchendaele. 'For him,' Rawle Knox would write, '"The Great War" was a natural extension of his life, practically all activity interested him and this was more exciting than most . . . He had always been fascinated with guns.' Shepard ended up 'a pillar of Sussex society', as Milne would never be.

There were plenty of other candidates for the job of

illustrating Milne's children's poems. Looking at *Punch* for the year before the book came out, one sees E. H. Shepard's drawings of children as no better and sometimes rather worse than those of several other artists. The choice might easily have fallen on A. E. Bestall (who would become less famous for another bear, Rupert, when he took over Mary Tourtel's creation) or D. L. Ghilchik or G. L. Stampa. But Shepard turned out to be perfect in most people's eyes, though R. G. G. Price would speak of his bourgeois 'prettification' and Geoffrey Grigson (notoriously hard to please) of his 'splendid insipidity'. Milne himself was delighted from the moment he saw the first drawings Shepard did – the ones for 'Puppy and I', the poem that recalls a long-ago Gordon Setter, Brownie, who appeared out of nowhere just as the puppy does in the poem. The child and the puppy demonstrate admirably Shepard's particular pleasure in what Penelope Fitzgerald has called 'the characteristic movement of the design from right to left'. It was the feeling of life, 'the tension of suspended movement', in Shepard's drawings that made him so outstanding when he was doing his best work.

One critic would say that Shepard's illustrations belong to the verses 'as intimately as the echo does to the voice'. Certainly, the extraordinary success Milne would enjoy owed a good deal to Shepard, but any suggestion that it was because of Shepard can be easily dismissed when one looks at the long-forgotten books of children's verse Shepard would also illustrate delightfully in the next few years, such as Georgette Agnew's *Let's Pretend* and Jan Struther's *Sycamore Square*. A lot of people would try to jump on the merry-go-round. One can't help wondering what Milne felt as he read E. V. Lucas's own contribution *Playtime and Company* (published a year after Milne's first poems), complete with Shepard's Pooh-like bear on a bed, a Christopher Robin lookalike and even a poem about rice pudding, with these strange lines addressed to the reluctant nursery eater:

> *When you next the pudding view,*
> *Suppress the customary 'Pooh!'*
> *And imitate the mild Hindu.*

Milne with Bestall or Ghilchik might easily have had the same impact as Milne and Shepard. Shepard without Milne nearly always sank without trace, unless he were illustrating, as he would, books that were already established, such as (to Milne's great pleasure) new editions of *The Wind in the Willows* and *Bevis*.

Milne came to acknowledge fully how much he owed to Shepard, but, at the end of 1923, he was worrying mainly about a title for the series of poems that were to appear in *Punch*. He wrote to Owen Seaman: 'They want a general title and I can think of none better than *When We Were Very Young*, but I am ready to be persuaded if you, or anybody, can suggest something. *Children Calling* was my only other idea, but Uncle 2LO has made that vulgar.' Seaman was obviously not quite happy about *When We Were Very Young* because Milne, a few days later, sent a list of further suggestions:

Alternative titles:

A Nursery Window Box
From a Nursery Window (or Through the NW)
Pinafore Days
Swings and Roundabouts (probably been used before)
Buttercups and Daisies

I think the first of these is the best, but I am not sure that it is better than WWWVY.
My brain has given out, and I can think of no more.

It was Milne's own idea that the series should start off with three short poems, and they duly appeared, under the title *When We Were Very Young*, in *Punch* on 9 January 1924. They did not look very impressive. Unillustrated, they were rather squashed up together. First, 'Brownie', the one about the creature behind the curtain; then 'In the Fashion', the poem about tails; and finally 'Before Tea', where Emmeline has not been seen for more than a week, having gone off in a huff when someone told her her hands weren't clean. A week later 'Puppy and I' appeared as a full-page spread with E. H. Shepard's drawings, much larger than they would be in the book, surrounding the five stanzas. Milne would at one stage identify it as his own favourite of all the poems.

The other poems that would appear in this way were 'The King's Breakfast', 'Teddy Bear', 'Nursery Chairs', 'Lines and Squares' (including two pictures – one of a replete bear who has just finished tucking into a passer-by – which would not get into the book), 'Market Square' and 'Little Bo-Peep and Little Boy Blue'. There were others that appeared unillustrated – and then the whole series of twenty-five ended with another four full pages: 'The Three Foxes', 'Jonathan Jo', 'Missing' and 'Happiness' – the last again with extra pictures: John putting his boots on. Four more would appear in the American children's magazine *St Nicholas* during the summer and autumn. These were illustrated by Reginald Birch, who had become famous nearly forty years earlier for his drawings for a book which had made publishing history: *Little Lord*

Fauntleroy. Before we look at the similar extravagant reactions to the publication of *When We Were Very Young* the following winter, we should see what else had been affecting Milne in 1924.

The health of Ken, his brother, had been causing worry for some time. Ken's doctor had diagnosed tuberculosis (usually then called consumption), and in the spring of 1924 it was decided that he must resign from the Ministry of Pensions and leave Croydon for the country. At that time, when there were no effective drugs to fight the disease, there was great belief in the restorative power of fresh country air. Milne was in the middle of rehearsals of his new play *To Have the Honour* (written some time earlier) when he heard the news from his father that Ken was having to leave the Civil Service. He wrote immediately to propose they have lunch at the National Liberal Club, which he still used rather than the Garrick from time to time when he did not want to be sociable. He suggested that they should discuss ways and means. There would obviously be problems, with Ken's pension – only a third of his salary – entirely inadequate to support his four 'good and clever' children, all still in full-time education. In 1922, when Ken had been in Pretoria on a government mission, J. V. Milne had sent one of his friends a family photograph and commented affection-ately: 'Look at happy Maud – always the same.' Things would no longer be the same; Alan Milne would be a necessary tower of strength to his sister-in-law Maud for the rest of his life. In 1924 he wrote to his brother:

> *As a throw-out I suggest that you let me pay £100 a year each for the education of your children; i.e. £400 a year now, £300 when Margery is settled, and so on. But more important than this is yourself. You'll have to write now, and really to stick at it, whatever the disappointments. As a start. I think I could get O.S. to let you try your hand at review-ing books for* Punch. *Turley made over £200 last year from this. If you got on all right at this, then I think there might be other openings. The Editor of the* Nation *is rather well-disposed towards me at the moment, but I fancy that we should have to be able to quote* Punch *to him first. Of course one feels that 'any fool can review a book', which may or may not be true, but the mere feeling creates an enormous amount of competition – which is why I am butting in. For God's sake don't think I mean by all this: 'You've jolly well got to set to, and earn some money' – You know I don't; but I do mean,*

old boy, that you're only 43, and that it's no good regretting the brilliant service career which has been denied you, when there's another sort of career still open and waiting for you. There are dozens of good novels and plays waiting to be written, and hundreds of articles; but a little regular reviewing would be a great help meanwhile, not only financially, but artistically. And you know that if I can help in any way, I will. My love to dear Maud. In a sneaking sort of way I envy you both going to live in the country!

Yours ever affectionately,
Alan

By the summer, Ken and Maud were settled at Shepton Mallet in Somerset. 'He is very brave about it all,' his father commented, describing how Ken sleeps 'out of doors, in one of those revolving shelters and at 7.30 Maud comes in her dressing-gown with their early tea,' across the damp grass. There had been some talk that J. V. Milne might join them in Somerset – he would miss them sorely in south London – but 'Maud will have all her work looking after Ken.' There was no suggestion that Daphne would tolerate her father-in-law.

From now on, until Ken's death, there are regular

letters from Alan, seeking to cheer and entertain his brother in his rural isolation, so that we know far more than we would otherwise have done, if Ken had remained in London, about Alan's activities during the years of publication of the four children's books. Several times Milne invited Ken to visit them in the country. Whether he went or not we do not know. Christopher could not remember meeting his uncle. Occasionally Alan would go down to Somerset (never with Daphne), occasionally at the beginning Ken would come to London (sometimes with Maud); sometimes there would be telephone calls ('Maud's voice on the telephone did me a lot of good, and made me feel much nearer to you both'); sometimes Alan would meet the children off trains. But for the most part there were just the letters, often long.

Alan treads a delicate tightrope, knowing how interested his brother is in what is going on, wanting him to know how much money is coming in, so that he can realise how easily Alan can afford to help him (this year Tony had considerable medical expenses, which Alan cheerfully paid, when the boy's appendix flared up) – but not wanting to seem to boast or to make it difficult for Ken to accept. It is always harder to receive than to give, as Christopher Milne too would find. ('I am bad at receiving, bad at having to be grateful.') It seemed particularly hard for Ken that the bitter end of his own career should have come just before the time of Alan's greatest triumphs.

But in April 1924 Milne was having a terrible time with Gerald du Maurier during rehearsals at Wyndham's of *To Have the Honour*, struggling to get him to produce it 'in the proper fantastic-comedy spirit'. How Du Maurier must have loathed the interfering author. Milne was relieved to get down to the rented cottage at Poling in May. At least the reviews were reasonable. It was, *The Times* decided, 'Mr Milne at his lightest. The fun is in the details and you don't trouble yourself over much about the story.' It would have its 150th performance in September.

But, as usual, there were people longing for Milne to do something bigger. The *Illustrated London News* critic begged him to 'drop his masquerade and forget to be polite'. It was all very well for him to poke gentle fun at the British love of rank and titles, but, the critic suggested, he should 'use his splendid gifts in serious satire, to be less gracious and more in earnest, for we have sore need of his talents.'

On the same page as the review of 'The New Milne Comedy' the magazine carried a picture of 'The First Labour Premier and his daughter as guests of the King and Queen at Windsor'. Milne started at about this time a habit he would continue for the rest of his life of writing letters to *The Times*. A few months earlier the General Election had ended in a stalemate – the Tories with 258, Labour with 191 and the Liberals with 159. When the final outcome was still in the balance, Lord Hawke, well known as a cricketer (captain of Yorkshire for many years) had written to *The Times* appealing to the Tories and the Liberals to form a coalition to keep Ramsay MacDonald out. Milne could not resist drawing Hawke's attention to an interesting precedent:

> *Lord Hawke, horrified at the political prospect, makes a despairing appeal 'from a sportsman's point of view' to Messrs Baldwin and Asquith. From the same point of view, I make an appeal to him. I remind him, in short, that not only was Australia ruled by Labour for many years without detriment to the Empire, but that it was actually under a Labour government that she won the last Test Matches, and under a Coalition Government that we lost them. I would ask him, therefore, to consider, before he commits himself to a new coalition, whether the prospects for 1924–1925 are really as desperate as he imagines.*

This rather teasing letter is indexed solemnly by *The Times* as 'on possible Labour ministry'; and the possibility, as we know, became an actuality. Ramsay MacDonald, with the support of the Liberals (determined to keep the Tories out of office) formed the first Labour government. There was a generally jumpy attitude to the new government. Milne must have smiled wryly at one particular cartoon in *Punch*, where a golfer groans 'I'm dead tired tonight' and his wife tries to cheer him up with 'Never mind, dear, perhaps the Labour government will abolish golf.'

Late in the year, just at the time of the publication of *When We Were Very Young*, Milne was enraged by a letter from the Bishop of Gloucester in *The Times*, written on board the Cunard liner *RMS Berengaria*, complaining because he could no longer afford to keep three gardeners. No wonder, he said, that there is so much unemployment when everyone is pricing themselves out of the market. The Bishop also bewailed the way the lower classes wasted their money. Milne adopted a highly satirical tone in his reply:

> *It is refreshing to find that the higher clergy are as human as ourselves, and one sympathises with the Bishop of Gloucester's feeling that if his income tax were lower, and if he could employ three gardeners*

for the price of two . . . not only would he himself be happier, but that a reflected glow of happiness would probably spread itself over the rest of the community. We have all felt like this from time to time.

But upon one point in his letter I ask for further enlightenment. He writes of the wealth which, by the lower classes, is squandered on 'the pictures' and charabancs as 'economically an unprofitable employment of labour'. From one of our spiritual instructors this is a little surprising. What does he hold to be the reason of our existence – the provision for each other of bread and boots, or the development of our souls? Agriculture, he insists, is a 'profitable' employment of labour, presumably because the product of it is not 'wasted' – it helps to keep us alive? But why are we keeping alive? Apparently in order to make boots and build houses for each other – good, profitable employment. Profitable employment in short, is employment which benefits the body; unprofitable employment, squandered money, is that which is devoted to the soul. Strange teaching for a Bishop! The pictures and charabancs, poetry and painting, the view from Richmond Hill, and the silence of a Cathedral, a concert and a day in April, these things, like education, were admirable when the

*country was wealthy; but now, with the wages of
gardeners what they are, money spent on them is
money wasted. Is this indeed what the Bishop wishes
us to believe? and are there never moments when he
understands that 'pictures and charabancs' are not
merely profitable, but the only profitable things in
life? I seem to remember a text . . .*

'Man does not live by bread alone.' It was the same argument Milne had used years before to justify the life of the writer, the artist. But did he ever have a sneaking feeling that plays like *The Dover Road* and *To Have the Honour* (good entertainment, certainly; enjoyable, apparently) were not exactly developing anyone's soul? Did he read *The Waste Land*, which had just been published, and admire it? Probably not. But he went to see Sybil Thorndike in *Saint Joan* that year and perhaps felt a pang of envy. He certainly admired Shaw. In a letter to *The Times* Milne would say:

*Let us curse the present state of the theatre (or
whatever we call the managers who refuse our
plays) as heartily as we like, but don't let us wash
our hands of it with a superior air, and then look*

around for sympathy. That was not how Saint Joan
came into the lives of the half-crown public.

At Poling that summer (just about the worst summer on record; it was even wetter than Wales the year before) Milne wrote yet another light comedy: *Ariadne*. He described it in a letter to Ken: 'It is about a solicitor'; he knew about solicitors. He was still seeing something of his eldest brother Barry, who was one. J. M. Barrie was always saying how one should write about things one knows. But when it was produced in the spring of 1925, the reviews were very mixed and Milne was swearing once again never to write another play.

At Poling, between the acts and showers, Milne took photographs, and sent them to Ken. The captions included:

1) Child in pursuit of elusive cabbage-white. Nurse
saying 'He'll never catch it'; Mother saying, 'Surely
those are the Parkinson-Smiths over there.'
2) Child examining captured butterfly. Observe the
latter's antennae.

Milne sent that snapshot to Irene Vanbrugh, as well, boasting about the antennae and about the beauty of the child. It would seem to be the photograph so familiar from the cover of the Penguin edition of Christopher

Milne's own memoirs, but it is impossible to see the antennae. Milne wrote to Irene:

> *I bore all the Garrick with it and it is, by general consent, the most perfect photograph ever taken. You might think I was become rather an expert with the camera but I have to confess, Madam, that these things are largely a matter of luck.*

> *3) Child preparing Father's bran-mash for breakfast.*

In the absence of this actual photograph, we cannot be sure that this was really what the child was doing, mixing some ancestor of muesli, but it's a nice thought.

There were more than cabbage whites at Poling. Alan wrote about butterflies to Ken, remembering the far-off golden summer of 1892, when Ken had had *British Butterflies* as a birthday present. There were plenty of Red Admirals and Peacocks in Sussex in 1924, 'but the Painted Lady seems to have died out since our day and we've only had one Brimstone.'

The best thing in the summer of 1924 was that, after a considerable search, the Milnes found the country cottage they had been looking for. Irene Vanbrugh was in New Zealand when Milne wrote to tell her about it. 'New Zealand is the one country in the world I envy you.'

He would say something similar in a reply to a fan letter years later, 'I always suspect the others of being full of the worst kind of insect, Kangaroos that kick you, and other unpleasant beasts . . . We get possession (delightful word) in October', but it was 'more or less derelict before we came'. There was so much to be done it would be well into the spring of 1925 before they would be able to use it. Milne called it a cottage, but it was actually an old farmhouse – sixteenth-century perhaps, parts of it even older. It was known as Cotchford Farm and was near Hartfield in Sussex, halfway between Tunbridge Wells and East Grinstead, on the borders of Ashdown Forest.

This is the Forest where, not long afterwards, Winnie-the-Pooh would take up residence 'under the name of Sanders' and E. H. Shepard, drawing the actual places, would add a new landscape to the imaginations of readers all over the world who had never set foot in the forest. Shepard's impression of Cotchford Farm itself is in the background of 'Buttercup Days' in *Now We Are Six*, with Christopher and his friend Anne Darlington, to whom the book is dedicated, in the foreground.

In October, Alan sent Ken a photograph of the house, with a detailed description of the alterations. They were building on a servants' hall adjoining the kitchen with, over it, 'a dressing-room for me next to Daff's bedroom'.

They were converting attic rooms into servants' bedrooms and making 'a sort of ping-pong playroom for him and us'. The chief sitting room was a splendid room. Milne called it 'the most lovely room in the whole world', with a huge fireplace in the middle of it and French windows out on to a lawn – then overgrown – running down to a stream. They were converting a barn into a garage with a flat over it. Alan was taking his father down to see it the following week, but, for the most part, it felt, as the builders worked on it, tantalisingly out of reach. The Milnes were merely poring over seed catalogues and dreaming of a time when there would be a resident gardener with a wife who, in their happy imaginations, would have a delicious meal waiting for them on Friday evenings, when they arrived for the weekend.

When We Were Very Young was published in London on 6 November 1924 and in New York on 20 November. Methuen placed an order with the printers, Jarrold of Norwich, on 17 September for a special edition of 110 large copies on hand-made paper and for 5,140 regular trade copies. On 18 November they ordered the printed endpapers (with nine of Shepard's small boys – called variously Percy, John and Christopher Robin – and one little girl, Emmeline) and these were first used in the second impression, which followed hot on the heels of the first, as that sold out on publication day. Milne had a royalty, of course, but Shepard had apparently accepted a lump sum of £50 for the illustrations, on top of what he had had from *Punch*. 'The next day Methuen decided to give me a cheque for £100 as a bonus,' Shepard remembered. They could well afford to do so. By the end of the year, less than eight weeks after publication, Methuen already had 43,843 copies in print. And John Macrae of Dutton's, who had published a fortnight later, was able to cable Milne for Christmas, saying he had already sold 10,000 in America. 'Not so bad,' Milne commented. He already had some confidence in the extraordinary potential of this slim children's book.

The cream paper jacket (which carried four more small boys, Little Bo Peep and the bear we now think of as Pooh) made much of the fact that this was a novelty from an already distinguished author:

Here is a departure from this popular author and dramatist's usual lines. He has always amused and delighted grown-up readers and playgoers; in this gay and frolicsome book he will enchant the nursery too.

Mr Shephard's drawings are in keeping with Mr Milne's irresistible fun and fancy.

Milne had first dedicated the book simply,

TO THE LITTLE BOY
WHO CALLS HIMSELF
BILLY MOON

but the final version (perhaps encouraged by Daphne) identified the child clearly not only as Milne's own son, but as the character in some of the poems. It reads:

TO
CHRISTOPHER ROBIN MILNE
OR AS HE PREFERS TO CALL HIMSELF
BILLY MOON
THIS BOOK
WHICH OWES SO MUCH TO HIM
IS NOW
HUMBLY OFFERED

Many adults undoubtedly bought the book for their own pleasure, but the papers invariably reviewed it as a children's book as the publishers intended. Most of them gave it a good deal of space, though the *Star* gave it only two lines 'between the *Chatterbox Annual* and *The Girls of St Monica's*' and the *Morning Post* headed its review 'Jingles for the Nursery' and continued in that vein 'to our utter disgust', Milne said. John Drinkwater's review in the *Sunday Times* was one of the most interesting. He told Milne beforehand that it would sell 'thousands of copies' – but 'whether of his books or mine' Milne wasn't sure before he read it.

Drinkwater made a strong distinction between 'the inventive fun' of the rhymes written 'for a young fellow called Christopher Robin' and the stuff which seems to have strayed in from any book of bad poetry for children 'into an extremely good one'. Drinkwater particularly disliked 'Twinkletoes' which 'had reduced even Mr Shepard to a level of ordinary fairy inanity'. Dismissing such poems as 'Water Lilies' and 'Spring Morning' and 'There's a cavern in the mountain where the old men meet' (all the ones that nobody remembers), Drinkwater spoke out for the arrival of 'a new prophet', someone fit to be mentioned in the same breath as Lewis Carroll.

Mr Milne's deftness is not to be questioned, but the fortunate thing is that it is, apart from the few lapses, always at work, as Lewis Carroll's was, on a sound common sense foundation ... Mr Milne treats his small companion as a sensible being who, indeed, wants to make up things, as is proper, but wants to make them up about real life and not about fairy doodleum. These two go about in the gayest and most whimsical of tempers, but the things that engage their attention are the soldiers at Buckingham Palace, the three little foxes who didn't wear stockings and didn't wear sockses, the gardener, the king who asked for no more than a little butter for the royal slice of bread ... It is all great larks, but I wonder whether the Sterner Critics will realise that it also is a very wholesome contribution to serious literature.

Milne would fortunately not live long enough to read the sternest critic of all, Geoffrey Grigson, fulminating about the book even while realising that 'few other poems have sold so enormously', not since Byron and Tennyson, anyway. Grigson would see Betjeman's debt to Milne. 'How is it that no one is asked, in Advanced Level English or even in the Tripos to estimate the influence' of Milne on 'Miss Joan Hunter-Dunn', for instance. But Grigson thought Milne's poems smug poems, poems for Us, marking us off from Other People – from titled people as well as the plebs, he observes, remembering Bad

Sir Brian Botany, who has to be cured of his arrogant ways and become one of Us as B. Botany Esquire. The children in the poems, he says, live in the right London squares and, if male,

> are earmarked for the better schools, then the better colleges, high on the river (*mens mediocris in corpore sano*), at one of the 'two' universities; and that male and female they come of families comfortable, secure, self-certain, somewhat above the middle of the middle class.

Are the poems for other children of such homes? No, rather than yes. Children, in my experience, of every generation since and including the Twenties, have found the poems nauseating, and fascinating. In fact, they were poems by a parent for other parents, and for vice-parental nannies – for parents with a war to forget, a social (and literary) revolution to ignore, a childhood to recover. When We – We – Were Very Young the book is named, after all, indicating its aim; which, like the aim of all natural bestsellers, was not entirely explicit, one may assume, in the author's consciousness.

Here mamas of the middle way, and fathers, and nannies, those distorting reflectors of the parental ethos, could be sure of finding Innocence Up to Date.

Little Lord Fauntleroy – here he was, stripped of frills and velvet (as we can tell by the splendid insipidity of the accompanying drawings) for modern, sensible clothes; heir, after all, to no peerage, but still the Eternal Child. No hint in these poems of children nasty, brutish and short, as Struwelpeter or Hilaire Belloc made them.

Are there ever tantrums, as these nice children say 'cos', and 'most', and 'nuffin', and 'purfickly', and 'woffelly', in their nice accent?

> What *is the matter with Mary Jane?*
> *She's perfectly well, and she hasn't a pain.*

If there were tantrums, it is rice pudding again; but not the child psyche, not infant sexuality, not Freud, who had now entered the pure English world.

The innocence of *When We Were Very Young* – of course it chimes with the last tinkle of a romantic innocence which by the Twenties had devolved to whimsy. Christopher Robin comes trailing the tattiest of wisps of a glory soiled by expectation and acceptance. The clouds have gone grey. The Child, in spite of Westminster and Trinity, is all too much at last the Father of the Man. And whenever the Child's impresario allowed an entr'acte, it came in parallel

modes of the expected and decayed – daffodowndil-
lies and the last fairies (inherited from the more
fanciful – and sinister – inventor of Peter Pan),
Twinkletoes upon the apple leaves, the Lake King's
daughter on the water-lilies, cave ancients tapping at
golden slippers for dainty feet, bluebells, and black-
birds' yellow bills . . .

These poems for people towards the top with children beneath the age of literary consent have the
qualities of rhythm, shape, economy, and games with
words – good qualities, after all. Would it be too pon-
derous to say as well that they were poems for a class
of middle to top people who had lost their intellectual
and cultural nerve, who expected of right things which
they had not earned, and who had scarcely looked a
fact in the eye for fifty years? It might be too ponder-
ous. But it would be true.

There is some common ground between the two poet
critics, writing exactly fifty years apart. They dislike the
same poems; they admire Milne's deftness, his technical
skill. The difference is mainly that Drinkwater was writing
at a time which took the class background completely for
granted, and indeed when the word 'whimsical' could be
used without pejorative undertones. Grigson, though born

into such a world, was unable to enjoy the verse for the sociology. He is nauseated, in fact, as many have been, not by the rhymes themselves, but by the whole paraphernalia of nannies and afternoon walks and clean hands for nursery tea. 'It's that bloody nanny,' Roald Dahl said to me, admiring Milne enormously and regretting how his books have dated. In fact, the nanny (or 'Nurse') appears in only five of the forty-five poems in *When We Were Very Young* and in another four in the second collection *Now We Are Six* – and, of course, not at all in the Pooh books.

Compton Mackenzie, writing in 1933, also saw the first book, above all, as a social document:

> *When We Were Very Young* marks an epoch as positively as any children's book has ever marked one. It is not extravagant to surmise that a distant posterity may find in that volume of children's verse a key with which to unlock the present more easily than with any contemporary novel, poem or play.

Yet if one reads the poems objectively, ignoring the charming period illustrations (many of which, surprisingly, have not dated all that much – look at the boy putting on his raincoat) the main impression is of a number of entirely natural children, egotistical, highly imaginative, slightly rebellious, as children still are. Certainly, as we saw at the beginning of this book, Milne's own memories of childhood, which play such an important part in the poems, have little to do with nannies and nurseries, and a great deal to do with adventuring, without adults, with freedom and growing independence. The children in the poems are always wanting to break free from the constraints that are constantly being imposed on all children, from whatever social background. ('Don't do that!' 'Come here.') Milne's children want to get 'up the hills to roll and play', to watch the rabbits on the common, to ignore the boring injunctions to 'Take care, dear' and 'Hold my hand'. They want to go down to the wood where the bluebells grow or to travel to South America or to sail through Eastern seas.

It is not a bland world. The menaces and uncertainties of real life are there all right, but perfectly adjusted to a small child's understanding. There are the bears waiting to eat the sillies who tread on the lines of the street. There are the Brownies hovering behind the curtain. There is the constant worry of pet mice, and mothers going missing – a fear, common in children, that the beloved animal may escape, that the person who goes out of the door may never come back. Bruno Bettelheim considers that the listening child can only enjoy the warning and has to repress the great anxiety that he will be permanently deserted. But the child in the poems is protected by his own egotism, is perfectly in control. Life goes on. ('If people go down to the end of the town, well, what can anyone do?') He would never be such an idiot as to tread on the lines; the bears are certainly not going to get him. There is a pleasurable thrill of danger, but ultimately a reinforced security.

The child answers politely all the endless grown-up questions (seething quietly inside) and thinks if only he were King of France he would not brush his hair for aunts. Indeed, if he were King of Greece, he would go so far as to push things off the mantelpiece. This seems to be a reasonable indication of three-year-old rebellion. The poems, in fact (and this is why they have lasted so long), are a true expression of the child psyche, as recognised by the child himself and as observed by his elders. They work both for children and for adults who can see through the class trappings to what is actually there. It helps too when one knows, as Grigson did not, that Milne did not come from a moneyed, smug background, or expect things which he had never earned. In fact, he was constantly worried by the established social order and the priorities of many of his readers, who were indeed very often just the sort of people both he and Grigson disliked and who took Milne's verses to their hearts. 'It is all most odd,' Milne reported to Ken. 'Yellow-faced Anglo-Indian colonels, with no livers and a general feeling that somebody ought to be shot down dammit sir, tell me with tears in their eyes how important it is to avoid the lines of the street and thus escape bears. And they light a long cheroot and tell anybody who is interested that they have knickers and a pair of braces.' And 'Pinero, of all people, patted me on the shoulder yesterday and told me what a wonderful book I had given the world. I don't suppose he has seen or read a play of mine in his life.'

It *was* all most odd. At Methuen there was a packers' strike and someone from the production department later remembered how he and every available person had volunteered to try to keep up with the demand as booksellers' orders for thousands of copies poured into the office every day. In America, the bookshops were taken totally by surprise by the demand. The initial advance orders taken had been for 385 copies. The critics were not particularly enthusiastic, but there are times, John Macrae of Dutton's would say, when 'the American public makes up its own mind'. By 1927, when *Now We Are Six* came out, they had sold 260,000 copies of *When We Were Very Young*. The demand owed a lot in the initial stages to the extraordinary enthusiasm of Macrae's son, who was then sales manager and sent copies of the book to anyone he thought would talk about it.

The letters of appreciation came pouring in – the first ones as a result of all the sales manager's free copies – from thirty-eight state governors, six members of the Cabinet, three Justices of the Supreme Court, eleven Rear Admirals, twelve Major Generals and everyone from Hendrik van Loon to Fred Astaire. One letter, headed F. Ziegfeld, New Amsterdam Theatre, New York, was from Lupino Lane and read like this:

> *I have to do an extra tumble tonight in the*
> *'Follies', slide down a flight of steps or jump*
> *through an extra trapdoor. Why, you ask? Oh,*
> *simply to express my exuberance over the fun I*
> *got in reading A. A. Milne's* When We Were
> Very Young.

Even President Coolidge was delighted, or so his secretary said.

Kermit and Theodore Roosevelt (sons of the former President) called in on Milne in London on their way to shoot tigers in Indo-Turkestan, 'a curious and delightful couple', Milne told Ken, 'all agog to have their copies of

When We Were Very Young signed. Kermit has got a first edition (English) and Theodore was almost in tears because he only had an American first edition.' They were very proud (not realising how little it would impress Milne) that a newspaper had published a verse about their projected hunting trip:

> *Kermit, Theodore*
> *Roosevelt, Roosevelt,*
> *Said to themselves, said they,*
> *There isn't a beast*
> *In Turkestan*
> *That we aren't prepared to slay.*

Everyone was quoting the poems and parodying them. A university wife in Kansas wrote to say 'No dinner with guests is complete without "Sir Brian Botany" or "James, James" or "Mr Teddy Bear". (You'd be surprised at the number of faculty people trying to reduce.)' Children at table no longer asked for butter but for 'some butter for the Royal slice of bread'. If anything was big, it was always 'enormouse'. And whenever something was lost, the cry would go up, 'Has anyone seen my mouse?'

A woman in Nashville, Tennessee, was typical of many who said that the poems appealed to all ages – her four-year-old 'found and recognised himself in almost every poem', but her eleven-year-old also loved 'The King's Breakfast', 'Bad Sir Brian Botany' and 'Three Foxes'. The most bizarre report was from the Hon. Edwin Samuel, who said he had read some Milne verses at a Jaffa Chamber of Commerce lunch. 'All those busy Arab merchants took the afternoon off for endless repeats of "Christopher Robin goes hoppity, hoppity, hop".' Everyone was hopping. A New York woman reported, 'We all had to hop. We kept it up until I was overcome by exhaustion and avoirdupois. Then just the children hopped.' They wanted to know about Christopher Robin. Does he really hop all the time?

An uncomfortable spotlight was already beginning to shine on the small boy himself. 'Grown-up readers as well as his contemporaries will thank him for helping to inspire the gay verses,' said someone on the *Sunday Herald Post*. The accompanying photograph of Milne showing a book to his curly-haired child, with a rather cool Daphne looking on, is captioned 'A. A. Milne, his wife and little daughter'.

The book was the subject of a leader in the *New York Herald Tribune*, in March, which quoted Coventry Patmore's 'The Toys' and said that 'pathos digs perhaps the most treacherous of pitfalls' when one is writing about children. 'Our own emotions get between us and the child's. It takes genius to identify itself with a child's blithe inconsequence ... Lewis Carroll had the gift. Stevenson had it ... Kipling when he wrote the *Just So Stories*. There are unmistakable signs of it in Mr A. A. Milne, the English playwright.' The paper suggested that anyone who didn't appreciate the book was a 'biffalo-buffalo-bison, who deserves to find treacle in his sockses'.

Milne wrote to E. V. Lucas on 3 April, saying 'It's in its 23rd edition in America! But of course not such big editions as you have been printing.' Sales escalated throughout the year, reaching a tremendous high with the run-up to Christmas 1925. 'Everybody's Talking about this Book', above a photo of Christopher Robin, was a headline in the *New York Telegraph* for November 1925, and in the following January the *Retail Bookseller* said that the sales record of *When We Were Very Young* 'is practically without parallel for any book in the last ten years'. It was generally agreed to be a book to put alongside Stevenson's *Child's Garden*, and A. A. Milne himself to be as 'quotable, contagious and personal an institution as Lewis Carroll'.

Milne pondered on the whole, extraordinary business. Before he had heard the mounting chorus of adulation, he had been a little irritated by Drinkwater's review which had 'a delightful air about it of how dare this fellow try to write poetry without a proper licence?' But could he now call himself a poet? If he found being a dramatist so horrible, what sort of writer did he want to be? A time would come when Auden would make a slightly ambiguous reference in his 'Letter to Lord Byron':

> Light verse, poor girl, is under a sad weather;
> Except by Milne and persons of that kind
> She's treated as démodé altogether.
> It's strange and very unjust to my mind . . .

Kingsley Amis, in the introduction to his *New Oxford Book of Light Verse*, noted Auden's 'good word' for A. A. Milne and quoted at length, and with tremendous approval, Milne's account of light verse in the course of an essay on C. S. Calverley, his old hero. Part of it echoes neatly Milne's account, in his autobiography, of writing for children:

> [It] is not the relaxation of a major poet in the intervals of writing an epic; it is not the kindly contribution of a minor poet to a little girl's album; it is not Cowper amusing (and how easily) Lady Austin, nor Southey splashing about, to his own great content, in the waters

of Lodore. It is a precise art . . . Light verse is not the output of poets at play, but of light-verse writers . . . at the hardest and most severely technical work known to authorship . . .

From time to time anthologies of light verse are produced. The trouble with most of the anthologists is that, even if they have an understanding of their subject, secretly they are still a little ashamed of it.

The same can be said of many writers for children. When the two come together, light verse written for children, there are some complex feelings going on, even as the writer looks at his extremely satisfactory bank balance.

Milne had done so much for Methuen's bank balance that in April 1925 they published a small collection of his adult light verse, *For the Luncheon Interval*, in card covers at one shilling and sixpence. It went into a second edition within the year, but no one regarded it as anything but a poor relation of the children's poems. Neither Auden nor Amis, when they came to make their light-verse anthologies, could find a single specimen of Milne to earn a place, though, curiously enough, Grigson did include 'Lines Written by a Bear of Very Little Brain' in his *Faber Book of Nonsense Verse*. Stephen Potter, in his exploration of the British sense of humour in 1954, suggested that there had been a revulsion against Milne by his generation, almost because he seemed then, in the early 1920s, 'so deliciously funny', with the funniness 'toppling over into sweetness and niceness'. The second half of the twentieth century prefers its humour blacker, less nice.

Milne would go on speaking out for comedy to be taken as seriously as tragedy, for light verse to be taken as seriously as serious verse. After all, 'in modern light verse the author does all the hard work, and in modern serious verse he leaves it all to the reader . . .' But he would gradually have to accept that it was only as a writer for children that anyone would take him seriously. In a poem in *For the Luncheon Interval* addressed to his nephew Jock, Barry's elder boy, and written long ago, in 1909, Milne had brooded on

> *we, who bear your name;*
> *Content (well, almost) with the good old game*
> *Of moderate Fortune unrelieved by Fame.*

He had now won, in no small measure, both Fame and Fortune. Whether they would make him content was another matter.

*

Drinkwater sent him his review copy to be autographed and Milne amused himself by parodying 'Happiness' in the front of it:

> John has a
> Great Big
> Actor-proof
> Play on,
> John has a
> Great Big
> Mayfair flat . . . etc. etc.

He gave him a bit of 'The Christening' too:

> I sometimes call him Terrible John
> 'Cos his plays go on –
> And on . . .
> And on.

It served him right for being so rude about 'Twinkletoes'.

Four days after the Drinkwater review, another book was published: *Fourteen Songs* – verses from *When We Were Very Young*, set to music by Harold Fraser-Simson, Milne's neighbour in Chelsea. When the poems were coming out in *Punch*, Milne had been approached by all sorts of composers wanting to set them to music. At one stage it seemed as if Frederic Austin, who had been on the wet

Welsh holiday, would do them, and Walford Davies was also keen. But Milne decided on Fraser-Simson, then immensely well known for his record-breaking musical *The Maid of the Mountains*. (A selection from that had been played at the New Theatre before the first act of *Mr Pim Passes By*, back in 1920.) One reason, apparently, was that Billy was extremely fond of the Fraser-Simson's liver-and-white spaniel, Henry Woggins; they often met on their daily walks. It was the beginning of a long collaboration – in the end there were sixty-seven songs. 'The music is exactly right,' Milne wrote to Curtis Brown. Not that he knew much about music.

Milne's story behind the dedication of *Fourteen Songs* is worth telling:

It was dedicated (by the composer of course)

By special permission of
H.R.H. Princess Mary
Viscountess Lascelles

to

Hon. George Lascelles
Hon. Gerald Lascelles

This was really Methuen's idea (E. V. Lucas being thick with Royalty just now), but there

is a limit to the number of Lascelles possible
in a dedication, and I suggested – if they had
to be dragged in –

> *By permission of H.R.H. . . .*
>
> *to*
>
> *The Autocrats of her Nursery*

– which has been allowed. But I really don't
know why we drag in Princess Mary at all. A
much more popular dedication would be:

> *By permission of*
>
> *'Mr A'*
>
> *to his illegitimate children*
>
> *in every clime*

This was in a letter to Milne's brother Ken. 'Mr A' was a
source of constant interest and speculation at the time.
He was, in fact, Sir Hari Singh, whose financial dealings
and involvement with a Mrs Robinson were making
headlines in the papers. A few days later Milne wrote:
'The bother is that it's no good telling you now who "Mr
A" is, but of course I knew weeks ago . . . God how I see
life . . . Mrs Robinson has refused an offer to appear on
the films, but will merely write her life for the papers

instead. I want to stand on tip-toe and scream.' The Lascelles dedication of the extremely successful book of songs – and a further dedication in the second book of songs to the Princess Elizabeth (the present Queen) – added to the feeling that Milne was somehow the Top Children's poet, and added to the hostile reaction that was beginning to be felt in some quarters. (Stephen Spender, for instance, whose parents had apparently been keen on keeping him from children who were rough, would later speak of the 'pure horror' of Christopher Robin.) Most people probably thought the dedication wholly appropriate and Milne kept his own feelings about royalty to himself most of the time. But on one occasion he could not help speaking out. He was dining at a private house and one of the other guests was Princess Marie Louise, granddaughter of Queen Victoria. It was she who had organised the Queen's Dolls' House not long before and she was graciously interested in A. A. Milne, whose tiny leather-bound 'Vespers' was in that exclusive library. 'I talked to her for about an hour after dinner, said "Ma'am" as little as possible, put my foot in it once or twice probably, withdrew it with a loud sucking noise and continued cheerfully.' The princess was foolish enough to lament to him 'the objection to work shown by the lower classes'. Milne swallowed and murmured that, indeed, 'every one of my friends would rather win £50,000 in a sweepstake than by working for it'. It was the best he could do on the spur of the moment. Her Royal Highness could perhaps hardly believe that the man she was talking to, whom, of course, she had supposed to be a gentleman, was identifying himself and his friends with 'the lower classes'. Milne reported to Ken, 'She didn't say anything, but a faint twinge of pain seemed to pass across her face, as if the first violinist were playing out of tune. Very sad.'

Milne could also speak out clearly on the golf course. One of his opponents, making the usual assumption that Milne would be a right-thinking supporter of the right, was grumbling about the government. 'What we need is a Mussolini,' he declared, and was somewhat discomfited when Milne replied coldly, 'Oh, do you like murderers?' Milne also showed where he stood, 'on the side of the people against privilege', in a review in the *Nation* of a collection of the cartoons of the left-wing David Low, which had a text by Rebecca West, writing under the name of Lynx. When he wrote, Milne did not know the identity of Lynx and assumed her to be a man:

Perhaps I am prejudiced, for Lynx's way of thought happens to be similar to mine . . . One follows behind

Low with a fearful joy, knowing that the next top hat
is for it, yet wondering just how; but one precedes
'Lynx' confidently after a little, saying over one's shoulder, 'Come on, there's a man in white spats over here,
absolutely made for you . . .' To Low's pencil Birken-
head and Thomas are equally comic, Bennett and
Belloc equally worthy of deflation; but 'Lynx' separates
the sheep from the goats and, if for the most part, his
pens bear the labels which I had long given them in
my own mind, I at least have no cause to complain.

Milne even began to think that he was Lynx himself, so
closely did he identify with this writer 'from the New
Statesman school'. In his review he does not mention the
description of his own plays, which cannot have been at
all to his taste and makes his praise of the book all the
more generous and interesting. After praising his children's books, Rebecca West went on to say:

And when he turns to what is professedly his adult
work he really does not move out of the nursery. What
gives his plays their curious sense of eeriness which
exists however matter-of-fact the content may be, and
their unaccountably touching quality, is our feeling that
somehow the limitations of age have been transcended

and we are watching the British child, its fair hair beautifully brushed, its eyes clear, its skin rosy, well trained, sweet-natured, very truthful and knowing no fear at all save that there may perhaps be some form of existence which is not the nursery and will not be kind however good one is, looking at life.

And, in the meantime, the yellow-faced Colonels and shingled hostesses clamoured to clasp him by the hand and gush over his book, misled, as Grigson would be years later, by the superficial trappings, into thinking that Milne was a contented, smug and fully paid-up member of the Establishment.

4

THE BEGINNINGS
OF POOH

In the midst of the acclamation for *When We Were Very Young*, and over the triumphant years to come, Alan Milne had to face over and over again his brother's sadly contrasting situation. Ken was following Alan's advice. Saving his strength in Somerset, he was trying to write. But he was intensely aware of how much he walked in his younger brother's shadow. Writing about his dog, Pete, for *Punch*, he could not help remembering Alan's pieces on another dog, Chum, years earlier. Alan tried to reassure him, before he had seen the article: 'I am sure it derives from Pete and not from me.' When it was published on 10 December 1924 (as the third impression of Alan's book had already been ordered) he wrote to Ken:

Dear boy,

1000000000000 congratulations on Pete. *It is admirable. Is it cheek if I say that I never suspected you of it? It is so damnably unforced; so leisurely; so mature; so – everything that it ought to be. The ghost of Chum salutes you: I strongly suspect him of saying sadly 'Yes, that's how my man ought to have done it.'*

Give Maud my congratulation. I hope she is proud of you. In point of style it is miles ahead of the ordinary Punch *article. Buy another piece of blotting paper, and stick to it. And I should be inclined to say 'Stick to* Punch'. *If you write about your left boot like that Seaman couldn't refuse it.*

Your very happy

A. A. M.

Ken would also, thanks to Alan, eventually do some regular reading for Methuen, though they were not encouraging at first. Alan tried to cheer him. 'There are so many available for this sort of work that other things than ability must count: proximity, for instance. Or some other case, even harder than yours, may have turned up.' At last, they did take Ken on and Alan was able to pass on an appreciative report from E. V. Lucas: 'You can tell your brother we regard him as a very valuable ally. He is so quick and decisive.'

In January 1925, Milne wrote to Maud with news of 'a new consumption cure' in Denmark. It was undoubtedly 'genuine: hallmarked by the *Lancet* and the *B.M.J.*'. He urged her to persuade Ken to try it, or at least to send the preliminary reports and X-rays, which would allow the Danish doctor to decide whether to take the case on for the eight-week cure, or not. Alan offered not only to cover all the expenses involved, but even to put up with the certainty of seasickness on the North Sea in winter and to cross with him. But he was determined not to badger Ken about his health or, 'so far as I can help it, have him badgered'. He just needed Maud to know how much he wanted (and how much he wanted he seemed hardly to be able to bring himself to say) Ken to take every chance there was of a cure. He said to Maud that he realised Ken might feel, 'Leave me alone – I'm sick of doctors': and that was presumably how Ken did feel, for he never went to Denmark.

Milne did not know quite what to do with himself in these early days of 1925, as the sales of *When We Were Very Young* continued to mount. He tried a novel, wrote the first chapter in the hope that the other chapters would write themselves, but 'some of these novels don't seem to try', he told Swinnerton. There were lots of invitations. Sometimes he was forced to meet people he found even more rebarbative than the Princess Marie Louise. He loathed Michael Arlen. 'He is in our eighth hell,' he told Ken. 'Above or below Gilbert Frankau?' He couldn't decide.

There were lots of letters to write. Daphne seemed to be losing the interest she had had in being Alan's secretary masquerading as 'Celia Brice'. There usually seemed to be other things she would rather be doing. Alan himself had always been bad about clearing his desk. In March, Chatto and Windus sent him an agreement for the publication of *Four Plays*. When the manuscript arrived in December, Swinnerton, his editor, had to beg for the counterpart agreement. 'Its twin, resting here, is becoming blurred with grief and yellow with age.' Milne liked getting letters. He told one fan: 'Letters like yours are the best part of the game'; but it wasn't, of course, quite the same when they had to be answered.

Probably the fan letter that moved him most was from Rudyard Kipling. He replied, 'If you can remember what you once said to Tennyson, you will know what your letter makes me want to say to you. I am proud that you like the verses.' Kipling had said to Tennyson: 'When a private is praised by his General he does not presume to thank him, but fights the better afterwards.' Only to Kipling himself would Milne have repeated such an analogy.

He was watching a certain amount of sport – rugger at Twickenham, the Boat Race – and playing a great deal of golf. His handicap was 'now officially 9, fortunately for our domestic happiness'. As long as Alan's handicap was in double figures, 'Daff hardly dared to mention it in polite society'. Daphne's feelings really did matter to Alan – on all things, great and small. She was very powerful. In this same letter, Milne joked, referring to himself and the four-year-old Billy, 'We men are in a minority.' Daff and he were laughing together over P. G. Wodehouse's lament in *John o' London's Weekly* over the decline of the old English sport of hawking. It was all golf nowadays.

Golf and the world golfs with you;
Hawk and you hawk alone.

Alan Milne boasted to Ken (who was still able to play a gentle game himself) of going round Addington in 84, including an 8 at the last, where he lost a ball. He went round Walton Heath in a satisfactory 85, though it was

about the most difficult course in London, with heather a foot high on each side of a narrow fairway, and a perpetual wind. I play a terrible lot of golf now – always twice and often 3 times a week, and it's really time I settled down to work again. But I don't know what. There is a perpetual murmur of 'Detective Story' going on in everybody's brain but mine: Daff's, Curtis Brown's, Methuen's, Dutton's (my American publisher), Hearst's (who want the serial rights), Mr A's (probably) and the Lord Mayor's.

Ken sat at home in Somerset listening to an actress called Rita Ricardo reading 'The Three Little Foxes', 'The Dormouse and the Doctor' and 'The Christening' over 2LO, on the 'wireless installation' that Alan had given him. And he read Alan's long letters. Alan told him Billy was learning to count. When his father, hearing 'One – Two – Three', asked him how far he could go, he said with surprise, 'Up to the end.' It was an answer that appealed to the latent mathematician in Milne. The boy was also learning to read and write:

> *He autographed a copy of his book for somebody yesterday. Entirely by himself – except that he had to be told what letter came next . . . The silly woman had written asking for his 'mark' – for a X – Bah! We Moons are a cut above that at 4¼.*

Milne discussed the child's feelings about the book in a letter to Lady Desborough, whom he had met a few times and who had written him a fan letter:

> *At the moment (4¼) Christopher Robin is a man*
> *of action rather than a man of letters, and I doubt*
> *if the book makes the appeal to him which it does to*
> *more studious natures . . . But he quotes from it*
> *sometimes; and, indeed, just to hear him call it 'My*
> *book' is happiness enough.*

'Just now he has the Meccano craze (and so have I as far as I am allowed),' Milne wrote to Ken. The boy also had a passion for drawing and painting. In February of 1925 he produced his masterpiece, which he told his father was 'St. George and the Dragon'. Milne wrote, 'It is of the Impressionist School. Daff and I were admiring it publicly and privately indulging in a little discussion as to some of the details. Billy meanwhile was finishing his lunch at the other end of the table, and, having finished it, said his grace to himself. This was it: "Thank God for my good lunch – and let those people understand the dragon." How well I know his feeling!'

Milne was not yet wary of allowing the child to become involved in the public reaction to the book. There was some discussion over whether to take him to the private view of an exhibition of Shepard's illustrations to *When We Were Very Young*, but that was probably because he might not enjoy the occasion. At this stage Milne's son had barely heard the words 'Christopher Robin' and most of the boys in Shepard's illustrations were certainly not him. Their hair was much shorter for one thing, though you couldn't always see it because of the hats. It was because of the dedication that it was his book; it was written for him. He was there, of course, in 'Hoppity', in 'Buckingham Palace', in 'Vespers' and in 'Sand-between-the-toes', and he felt he was there in some of the others. But he was not, like Tootles in *Peter Pan*, dazzled by being in a story. It all seemed perfectly natural. Daphne suggested it seemed no more extraordinary than it did to other children to find their pictures in the family photograph album. None of Milne's stories of Billy at this time suggest the shy creature of Christopher Milne's memories. It is impossible not to think that he was made shy, and his natural confidence eroded, by the attention he received in the following years. If Christopher Robin had played a minor part in *When We Were Very Young*, in the next book he would take a starring role.

The child's passion for St George and the Dragon determined one of his fifth birthday presents that summer:

a shining suit of armour. It is interesting that Christopher Milne's own story in *The Enchanted Places*, written nearly fifty years later, tallies exactly with the story Milne told at the time in a letter to Ken, a letter which Christopher never saw. Did he really remember so accurately or was it, more likely, a story his father often repeated?

> *As you know, he is very keen on dressing up, particularly as St. George v. Dragon. I was trying to teach him to catch last weekend, and he wasn't very good at it. I said, 'You must learn to catch, or you will never be any good at cricket. And you know when you're nine or ten, you'll think of nothing but cricket.' And he opened his eyes very wide and said 'Nothing but cricket? Not armour?' A dreary prospect opening up before him.*

The catching practice was going on at Cotchford, the farmhouse in Sussex, where the Milnes would now spend most weekends, as well as the Easter and summer holidays. Nanny would, of course, always go down with them. She would come in useful for fielding when it came to cricket, but it is remarkable how seldom Milne mentions her in his letters. She came between him and his son – there was no doubt about that – and he was jealous.

Christopher Milne would say that jealousy was his father's besetting sin. 'Jealous by nature – as I was too – more than anything he hated rivalry.' And Nanny – not Daphne – was his true rival for the love he longed for from his son.

Milne bumped his head happily on the low beams as he learned to live in the old house. He had a small, rather dark study with a window looking out across the front courtyard to the kitchen wing. Daphne had lavished a good deal of attention on the rest of the house, getting it just the way she wanted it, but it was in the garden that she really came into her own. There was something, it seemed, that she had always been wanting to do and that was to make a garden. She had a full-time gardener to help, but it was her garden and the picture we have of her in the country is very different from the image of her in London, with her hats and hairdressers and leisurely luncheons. 'She responded to the beauty, the peace and the solitude' that the country offered. 'She found this in the garden and she found it too in the countryside beyond. Solitude. She was happiest alone.' But their son would see Milne as 'a Londoner, a real Londoner with a deep love of London in his bones. For him the country had always been, not where you lived, but where you went. Where you went on holiday. Where you went to do something – to ride a bicycle, to climb a hill, to look for birds' nests, to play golf. Like a dog, he couldn't just be in the country, sitting or strolling aimlessly.' So Christopher would say, but once, in a novel, Milne himself would write that the good thing about the country is that you can do nothing there, because that means 'doing everything: thinking, seeing, listening, feeling, living'. But it was true enough that, like a dog, he was never happier than when chasing a ball. He needed someone to play with and Daphne hated all games.

So there was tiny Christopher Robin, still called Billy, being trained to throw and catch, an ancillary of his father. And there was Daphne, absorbed in planting and planning her garden. Their pleasure in their first 'picnic weekend' was rather spoilt when they returned to find there had been burglars in Mallord Street. Alan wrote to Ken:

> *Fortunately they were only out for the jewellery,*
> *and ignored all the silver spoons and forks. Still*
> *more luckily they searched every drawer in the*
> *house for Daff's jewel-case, and the actual case*
> *(which they probably thought was a tea-caddy)*
> *looked on and laughed at them. All they got was*
> *Two silver boxes*

Ciro-pearl necklace (which I hope they thought
was genuine)
   Jade and diamond brooch
   Ear-rings
   My gold wrist watch
   My gold 'albert' (which I haven't worn since 1914)
   and
   Two pairs of cami-knickers and two chemises of
Daff's! (You ought to have heard me describing the
cami-knickers to two stolid policemen.) About £70
worth. Insured, of course. The visitors came in
politely by the front door which they burst open with
a jemmy. They did no damage whatever inside,
owing to the lucky fact that not a single drawer,
cupboard or desk is ever locked in this house. But
bills, letters and clothes were scattered all over the
rooms. Holmes (or Gillingham) would undoubtedly
have said that they were really searching for the
secret will or the compromising photograph.

Gillingham was Milne's own amateur detective in *The*
Red House Mystery.

I have been interviewed by detectives, insurance
people, bloodhounds and what else, and have recon-

structed the scene of the crime a dozen times. There is
no doubt we shall get our money back all right.

The bulbs Daphne had planted on day trips from Chelsea
with sandwiches and a Thermos flask, when they had first
got possession in the autumn, were coming into flower
– hundreds of Darwin tulips that May. Just as Daphne's
role in Milne's writing was simply admiration and praise,
so was Milne's role, officially, in relation to Daphne's
garden. He admired very much what she and the gardener were doing, but perversely took even more pleasure
in the self-sown things, the flowers that sprang up of
their own accord – eschscholtzia, coreopsis, sidalcea and
aubretia. 'A cynic might say that my love is no more than
delight in an unearned, unexpected bonus. This is entirely
to misjudge me. It comes from a feeling that … this
unclaimed, unworked-for bounty is in some mysterious
way the product of my own idleness.' He did pull up an
occasional weed, priding himself on the length of its root,
and he wondered at the miracles of nature. 'That a nastur-
tium seed should take any further interest in life is the
most optimistic thing that happens in the world.'

The garden was Daphne's kingdom and Milne never
considered himself more than an under-gardener. In 1929
he would inscribe *The Secret* 'For Daffodil Milne' with

'the homage of the under-gardener'. But already in the summer of 1926 he would write, 'I am getting wildly keen on the garden, and slightly less unintelligent about it.' His own territory was the putting lawn and he was allowed to worry about the water. Water is always a worry as well as a pleasure. Its habits are quite unpredictable. There was a sort of ditch at the bottom of the garden, which tended to dry up in the summer. Later Milne would discover a spring and form a pond, which caused endless problems. It was perhaps something to do with chalybeate, the iron in the soil, or perhaps it was oil. Milne lived long enough to worry about the first explorations in the area by Sir Henri Deterding of the Royal Dutch Petroleum Company.

Across the ditch there was a meadow and beyond the meadow the river, a tributary of the Medway. They called it a river, though it was really only a stream, to distinguish it from the stream which was really a sort of ditch. The river was deep in a channel lined with alders. 'It was just the right width: too wide to jump, but where a kindly tree reached out a branch to another kindly tree on the opposite shore, it was possible to swing yourself over. It was just the right depth: too deep to paddle across but often shallow enough to paddle in and in places deep enough to swim.' It is of course the river, only Milne calls it a stream, in which Roo will squeak 'Look at me swimming!' and be rescued with the North Pole. Upstream, a short walk south-west of Cotchford, was the bridge, the scene of games of what would be called Poohsticks, and beyond the bridge was the forest.

'It is difficult to be sure which came first,' Christopher would write. Did they play the game Poohsticks before the story or only afterwards? It's such a natural sort of game, throwing sticks into a river and watching them come out on the other side of the bridge, seeing which one had won, that no one really needed to invent it. Probably there were already people playing it all over the world. But there would soon be many more.

And what was Winnie-the-Pooh, the teddy bear himself, doing all this time? He was certainly travelling the hour and a quarter each way, down with the others from Mallord Street to Cotchford and back in the new car driven by Burnside, the chauffeur. (Milne himself would drive, but on the whole he preferred to be driven. He drove 'terribly slowly and terribly badly', one of his nieces said, and he would later claim to be 'the only man in Sussex for whom cars did not start'.) And sometime about now – it is difficult to fix the exact moment – the bear acquired his highly individual name. He had already acquired a voice – 'Pooh's gruff voice as inspired by Moon', as Milne described it to Ken in 1928 when Billy had become Moon. Ten years or so later Milne said it was Daphne who had given the animals their voices. It was probably a bit of both. 'He and his mother gave them life,' Milne said. The child and his toy bear 'indulged in lengthy conversations', according to Daphne, 'Christopher interpolating fierce growls for the bear, feeling thoroughly convinced about it'. There was also some suggestion that the child would say things in a gruff Pooh voice which he knew would hardly be acceptable if he said them in his own.

The teddy bear himself played a very small part in the first book. Apart from his leading role in 'Teddy Bear', he makes only two very minor appearances in the illustrations. He had certainly not yet come into his own. If in physical form he was based on Graham Shepard's bear, in habits and domicile Teddy Bear (or more formally Mr Edward Bear) was certainly the Milne bear:

> *He gets what exercise he can*
> *By falling off the ottoman,*
> *But generally seems to lack*
> *The energy to clamber back.*

The ottoman was in Billy Moon's nursery on the top floor at Mallord Street, and the toys slept in there at night. The bear was the absolute favourite, the child's inseparable companion. Eeyore was already around (a present for Christmas 1921); he was a donkey with a drooping neck which naturally gave him a gloomy disposition. (Soon there would be a real donkey called Jessica in the thistly field beyond the Cotchford garden where later, after the animal's death, they planted a wood.) There was Piglet too, a present from a neighbour in Chelsea.

There have been many explanations of Winnie-the-Pooh's name, so many that it is a wonder Milne did not make a story out of them, in the manner of the *Just So Stories*. There is no question that the Winnie part came from a female Black Bear called Winnie (after Winnipeg), who was one of the most popular animals in the London Zoo during this period. (If you go to the Zoo now you can see a sculpture of a bear cub, which celebrates the link between them.) The real bear had crossed the Atlantic as the mascot of a Canadian regiment, the Princess Pat's, and had been left on Mappin Terrace in the safekeeping of the Royal Zoological Society in 1914, when the regiment went to France. She lived there until her death in 1934.

Christopher Milne certainly met this bear on more than one occasion. There are various accounts of how he reacted. His father, as reported by Enid Blyton, would say 'the bear hugged Christopher Robin and they had a glorious time together, rolling about and pulling ears and all sorts of things.' It sounds rather hazardous. E. V. Lucas was a member of the Society and knew many of the keepers. Through him it was possible to open doors and gates not normally opened to the general public. Laurence Irving, Henry's grandson, told a story – which had wide circulation in a letter to *The Times* in 1981 – of a visit to Winnie, when he invited the children of two of his Garrick friends, A. A. Milne and John Hastings Turner, to join his daughter Pamela on her fifth birthday. Mrs Irving's version was that Pamela, who had a keen sense of smell, had exclaimed 'Oh pooh!' on meeting the docile beast; Daphne certainly told the story that Christopher had said the same, but with pleasure rather than distaste, having decided he liked the bear after some natural initial trepidation on meeting the huge if friendly beast. ('The girls held their ground, Billy wavered, retreated a step or two, then overcame his awe.') However, the date of the expedition, so firmly fixed by Irving on his daughter's fifth birthday, makes it impossible that saying 'pooh!' to Winnie the bear at the Zoo can have had anything to do with the naming of Christopher Robin's teddy. Pamela was five on 22 March 1926, certainly seven months before the book was published, but three months after the first Pooh story had appeared in print.

Irving, writing to the paper so long afterwards, might well have confused the birthday. But the expedition cannot have taken place in March 1925, because it is also linked firmly with *Vaudeville Vanities*, a revue in which all three men – Irving, Milne and Hastings Turner – were involved. Irving had designed the sets for a rendering of 'The King's Breakfast', set to music by Fraser-Simson. It was an item which caused problems, as the producer felt sure that the Lord Chamberlain would object to the life-size cow's pale terracotta udders. Milne and Irving were both on the side of the udders – 'the source of the butter on which the plot depended'. *Vaudeville Vanities* opened late in 1926, after the publication of *Winnie-the-Pooh*. Indeed, if the visit to Winnie took place, as Irving says, 'during the long run of the revue', it must have been to celebrate Pamela's sixth birthday, in March 1927.

If I seem to have laboured this point it is because Irving's story has been much repeated. 'How did Winnie-the-Pooh get his name?' is a common question; it is such an odd name. Christopher Milne says 'I gave it to him' but nearly always uses just 'Pooh' and it is that part of the name that causes most problems. I have heard children, sadly, refuse to take the book off the library shelf 'because of its silly name'. A child psychotherapist was much taken with the fact that it was a swan that was first called 'Pooh' – a swan, in its pure whiteness, being the antithesis of the current association, in nursery language, with faeces. This association written without an 'h' – supposedly from the exclamation at anything smelly or disgusting – did not come into the language until the 1930s (according to Eric Partridge) and whether it has anything to do with Pooh Bear it is impossible to say. There is nothing smelly or disgusting about Pooh.

Really, it seems best to leave most of the explanation to A. A. Milne himself. He says that when they said goodbye to the swan at Arundel, 'we took the name with us, as we didn't think the swan would want it any more'. And when Edward Bear wanted 'an exciting name all to himself, Christopher Robin said at once, without stopping to think, that he was Winnie-the-Pooh. And he was.' Milne could not remember whether Winnie at the zoo was called after Pooh or Pooh after Winnie, but we know that that large Canadian bear was Winnie long before Christopher was born. Then there is the complication of the bear's sex and of the mysterious 'the' in the middle of the name. Milne again:

When I first heard his name, I said, just as you are going to say, 'But I thought he was a boy?'

'So did I,' said Christopher Robin.

'Then you can't call him Winnie?'

'I don't.'

'But you said—'

'He's Winnie-ther-Pooh. Don't you know what 'ther' means?'

'Ah yes, now I do,' I said quickly; and I hope you do too, because it is all the explanation you are going to get.

It only remains to remember that Pooh had such stiff arms, 'from holding on to the string of the balloon all that time that they stayed up straight in the air for more than a week, and whenever a fly came and settled on his nose he had to blow it off. And I think – but I am not sure – that that is why he was always called Pooh.' Well, it's possible.

And as for it not being possible for a male creature to be called Winnie, it is just worth wondering whether Pooh helped Churchill's nickname during the war and reinforced his tubby reassuring image when Britain stood alone.

In the spring of 1925 Winnie-the-Pooh was still a toy bear and not a book. He was not even in a story. But after the success of the poems, everyone forgot about the detective story and started pressing Milne to produce another children's book. *When We Were Very Young* was already firmly established as 'the greatest children's book since Alice'. Indeed, its rare status had been acclaimed immediately on publication: 'It is a book that all children will adore. It is a book that mothers and nurses will laugh and cry over. It is a – classic!'

Carl Pforzheimer, an extremely rich book collector, began as early as 1925 to build up the collection of manuscripts, typescripts and Shepard pencil sketches which would eventually, after his death, sell at Sotheby's in London in 1986 for £120,000 ($180,000). Milne obviously thought at this stage that his success might not last and he should cash in on it while he had the chance. Later he regretted very much that he had let the material go; he would be more careful in future.

Milne had always prided himself on his financial astuteness, but he made another mistake in 1925. An American publisher, David McKay Co. of Philadelphia, wanted him to write some stories to go with some paintings by an artist called H. Willebeek Le Mair. On 29 March, Milne wrote to Curtis Brown, 'At present am still wrestling with the McKay pictures. As soon as any sort of book begins to heave in sight, of course I will let you know.' As he was merely adding some words to a set of existing pictures, he foolishly agreed to a lump payment with no royalty. The *Bookman* said, 'If you like Mr Milne's verses, you will like his stories . . . They all come from the same mint.' But posterity (and Milne himself) distinguished the wheat from the chaff. A recent critic said *A Gallery of Children* 'intrudes like a pale white slug between two butterflies' – but it sold on the strength of Milne's name. He wrote to a friend in November: 'For God's sake don't buy it. I sold the thing outright to an American publisher – in a moment of madness – for £200. He has already sold 50,000 copies at 3½ dollars. Take 10% on that and you perceive that I have thrown away thousands.' He told Ken that 'McKay had the nerve to write and say that he looked forward to doing another book with me – verses with Shepard illustrations he airily suggested – on which he would "be willing to pay a royalty". I told him to go to San Francisco and chew gum.'

Milne *was* working on more verses. He wrote to Curtis Brown in April 1925: 'Yes, I am prepared to do a dozen more verses of the *When We Were Very Young* kind for serial use in the next year if you can make a deal with the Hearst people.' Harper's offered 'up to £100 for 12 verses' but Milne argued for fifteen guineas each, and got that. He had actually had twenty guineas at Easter for a poem in the *Star*, 'and America is supposed to pay so much better than England'. He wrote to Ken:

> *Cassells are paying 200 guineas for the English*
> *rights of the twelve, provided that they average 30*
> *lines each.*
> *'The King asked –*
> *The Queen and – '*
> *Now you see the point of putting it out like this.*

He was encouraging Curtis Brown to insist on 25 per cent 'all through' when it came to his next children's book. What this would be he was still not at all sure. Certainly, he wanted to work with Shepard again, and indeed he had written to him early in 1925 to ask him if he would be interested in illustrating a new edition of *Once on a Time*, which had made so little impact when it was first published during the war.

> *My dear Shepard,*
> *Did you ever read a book of mine called 'Once*
> *on a Time'? No. However, I forgive you, as nobody*
> *else has. It was published – Hodder & Stoughton*
> *– in 1917, and died at birth. But until W.W.W.V.Y.*
> *I always thought it my best book.*

*And now, spurred on by our joint success,
H. & S. want to bring out a new edition,
illustrated by you. It is a long fairy story, and cries
aloud for my one and only collaborator. Will you do
it? H. M. Brock did it last time – 4 full pages, bad;
and 20 chapter headings, not bad. If you would do
it, it really might have a very big sale next
Christmas. Hodder & Stoughton are writing to
you. Methuens were very keen to get it away from
them and publish it (with your illustrations, of
course), but H. & S. weren't having any.*

*I should like you to do it in the verse manner –
with decorations all over the place – but I don't
know what the publishers' idea is. Anyhow, it is a
book on which I have always been very keen, and
which I have always felt has never had a chance, so
you can understand how keen I am that you should
do it. It is full of Kings & Princesses and dragons
& other strange animals – and, in fact, shouts for
you. So come.*

But Shepard was presumably too busy. Everyone was
wanting him to do things. Milne hoped he might illustrate a gift edition of his old children's play *Make-Believe*
for Chatto and Windus (cashing in on his new fame as a

children's writer), but Shepard did not do that either. In 1925 Hodder and Stoughton brought out another edition of *Once on a Time* with delightful illustrations by Charles Robinson, Heath Robinson's elder brother, most famous for his illustrations of *The Secret Garden* by Frances Hodgson Burnett. When he was very young, he had decorated the first edition of Stevenson's *A Child's Garden of Verses* and it seems quite natural that someone would think of him now in connection with Milne, but in fact the Robinson illustrations for *Once on a Time* had appeared in America three years earlier. In spite of Milne's efforts, for he was immensely fond of it, no one ever took a great deal of notice of it.

For the next two years, for the first time for many years, there were no Milne plays on in London or New York. But the book which was to make far more impact than any play and even than the children's poems, was – though it seemed impossible at the time – not far off. Christopher's bedtime stories consisted largely of the stuff of fairy tales – dragons and knights, giants and princesses and so on. Milne knew, as most parents do, that it is no good making things too exciting at bedtime. In fact, the more boring the story is, the more quickly the child goes to sleep. Nameless knights and indistinguishable princesses did the usual sort of things – 'a completely contemptible mix-up' Milne called it. But occasionally there was one story that was a little different. It was a story about the child's bear and a balloon and some bees. And the bear, as we have seen, had recently acquired his very unusual name – Winnie-the-Pooh, that good name for a bear who had to blow flies off the end of his nose because his arms were too stiff to be useful.

Milne was much in the public eye at the end of 1925, as a result of the continually bestselling, continually reprinting *When We Were Very Young*. There was a large supplement to the Christmas *Bookman* – eight pages entirely devoted to Milne's life, his family and his work, with lots of compliments and lots of photographs. The writer concluded: 'If you look back at his early sketches, and over the lengthening line of his plays, you will feel that from the first to the latest, they are linked up and related to each other by a charm of personality which gives colour to them all ... The dominant note in everything he has written, for mature people or little folk, is a joy in all life and a spirit of youth that never survives in the foolish.' There was a photograph of Milne offering a toy penguin to a dubious three-year-old with the teddy bear standing on the sidelines; there was one by Marcus Adams of a rather cool five-year-old, 'Christopher Robin Milne, to whom *When We Were Very Young* is dedicated';

one of Shepard's illustrations to 'Little Bo-Peep and the Little Boy Blue' 'from the original drawing which now hangs in the nursery of Christopher Robin' – and an extremely striking portrait of 'Mrs Milne' in profile, by E. O. Hoppé.

Milne wrote to Ken on the day that Daphne had been to the studio. She had been there with him once or twice before, and on her return said:

D: *I didn't know he was so French. He used not to be.*
ME: *Well, of course he has got an accent on the 'e'.*
D: *Yes – well, it was very acute this morning.*

Daphne was actually revelling in all the fuss. She wrote at the end of one of Alan's letters to Irene Vanbrugh: 'We are all very well and happy and pleased with each other and everything else!' Alan wrote to Ken:

There is a new paper (for 'Mothers') coming out next month with a special feature, 'Nurseries of the Highly Nourished' or some such title – anyway, Billy leads the way in the first number. He and his nursery were photographed all ways up, and Daff was interviewed, and explained how important it was to combine firmness with kindness, and I said nothing, and – well, get it. I wish I could remember the title for you.

Milne could not get away from his fame – and he did not really want to – even when that month he had to do four days' jury service. ('I 'ate the Law' was his only comment on the case.) The day before he had signed five hundred copies of *A Gallery of Children* – a limited edition in England. He was glad to have the hundred guineas for the signing, not because he needed it, but because it was certainly rankling that he had been so stupid in accepting the lump-sum payment from the American publisher. The day after the case he had to sign a hundred copies of a special edition of *The King's Breakfast*, and when the jury retired to consider its verdict a fellow jurywoman produced *Not That It Matters* – a collection of his essays that had just gone into a 'new popular edition' – and she asked him to sign that.

A few days later Christopher – still Billy – and Daphne were involved in a theatrical occasion. Milne wrote to Ken on 11 December:

> *Billy is being a Holy Innocent (with 20 other children and Gladys Cooper) at a matinée on Tuesday. At a sort of committee meeting, attended*

*by parents of Innocents (Holy) to consider costumes,
Daff said 'Oh, no!' in a loud voice from the back of
the room when somebody suggested dark-grey
flannelette (or whatever it was) – whereupon she
was immediately elected Managing Director or
Wardrobe Mistress of the whole scene. The result is
that every ten minutes the telephone bell rings, and
some anxious if aristocratic mother is heard
imploring Mrs Milne to let her little darling wear
blue. Two of them have already been here – 'any
time Mrs Milne would see me,' they say humbly to
me – and throw themselves at Daff's feet. Even a
father – the Colonel of the Grenadier Guards, no
less – took up an insignificant position in the
drawing-room, while Daff issued orders. What
snobs parents are about their children!*

As all the preparations for the matinée went ahead, Milne
was racking his brains to think of a children's story for
the Christmas number of the *Evening News*. Daphne,
preoccupied with the Holy Innocents, assured him it was
easy and that all he had to do was to write down 'any one
of those bedtime stories'. Milne assured her it was not
easy and that they weren't really stories at all – all that
stuff about 'dragons and giants and magic rings'.

'Wasn't even one of them any good?' she pleaded. And then Milne remembered 'that there was just one which was a real story, about his bear'. He sat down and started writing:

> This is Big Bear, coming downstairs now, bump-bump on the back of his head, behind Christopher Robin. It is, as far as he knows, the only way of coming down-stairs, but sometimes he feels that there really is another way, if only he could stop bumping for a moment and think of it. And then he feels that perhaps there isn't. Anyhow, here he is at the bottom, and ready to be introduced to you. Winnie-the-pooh.

That was the first time he had written the words Winnie-the-pooh. (The 'p' is definitely small in the manuscript.) He went on writing until he got to the point where Christopher Robin asks, 'Is that the end of the story?'

> 'That's the end of the story.'
>
> Christopher Robin gave a deep sigh, picked his bear up by the leg and walked off to the door, trailing Winnie-the-pooh behind him. At the door he turned and said,
>
> 'Coming to see me have my bath?'

'I might,' I said.

'I didn't hurt him when I shot him, did I?'

'Not a bit.'

He nodded and went out ... and in a moment I heard Winnie-the-pooh – bump, bump, bump – going up the stairs behind him.

It was indeed a real story, with a beginning, a middle and an end. In the book, after Christopher asks, 'Is that the end of the story?' Milne says, 'That's the end of that one. There are others.' In December 1925 there weren't, but the first story 'became Chap I. The rest inevitably followed.'

Explaining all this he would say that he never wrote anything 'without thought of publication'. After all, he was a professional writer. He would also say that he was lazy, and needed 'somebody or something to set me off'. If Milne had not had such a keen sense of what would make a publishable story, it is easy to imagine (so great was his fame the *Evening News* would have printed anything) that the next children's book after *When We Were Very Young* might have been about yet more knights and 'dragons and giants and magic rings', rather than the entirely original adventures of one boy's bear.

On Thursday 24 December 1925 the main news headline in the *Evening News*, stretching right across the front page of the paper, read A CHILDREN'S STORY BY A. A. MILNE and under, in only slightly smaller letters, the two words CHRISTOPHER ROBIN. And then:

**Page 7 To-night –
To-morrow Night's Broadcast.**

A new story for children, 'Winnie-the-Pooh', about Christopher Robin and his Teddy Bear, written by Mr. A. A. Milne specially for 'The Evening News', appears to-night on Page Seven. It will be broadcast from all stations by Mr. Donald Calthrop, as part of the Christmas Day wireless programme, at 7.45 p.m. tomorrow.

The headline was above and in far larger print than GREAT STORM SWEEPS OVER DERBYSHIRE (WHITE CHRISTMAS OVER TWO THIRDS OF BRITAIN), LORD COBHAM'S MANSION ON FIRE and WHITES' DANGER IN TIENTSIN. On page seven there was another enormous banner headline right across the page, simply

WINNIE-THE-POOH.

The illustrations were not by Shepard, who had presumably been too busy. He had managed to do a rather splendid version of Milne's poem 'Binker', with a girl in the main role, which appeared the same month in *Pears' Annual*. The *Evening News* illustrations for the story were by J. H. Dowd. Winnie-the-Pooh, not yet looking quite himself, had started his public life. He was on his way to becoming 'the most famous and loved bear in literature'.

5

WINNIE-THE-POOH

In January 1926, Milne wrote to Ken with a long list of 'things which ought to be done'. They included:

1) *A book of verses (about 15 done to date) to appear in*
   1927 or 1928, but they have to be done fairly soon, so
   as to be illustrated and then serialised (horrid word)
   in America. [This would be Now We Are Six.*]*
2) *A book – at Daff's and Billy's special request –*
   of Winnie-the-pooh. 2 done. The Evening News
   one, and one for Eve *in February.*
3) *A book of short stories I want to get out some time.*
   There are about 6 available and I want to do some
   others – am, in fact, in the middle of one now –
   grown-up ones, of course. [This would be The Secret
   and other stories, but it contained only four stories
   and appeared in 1929, in a limited edition only.]

4) *Playfair thinks I'm doing a pantomime for the Lyric, Hammersmith next Christmas, but I think I'm not.*

5) *I am doing an introduction for a collected edition of* Saki [The Chronicles of Clovis, *1928*].

6) *Proofs of* Four Plays *to correct.*

It was not actually a very substantial or demanding list, at least not for someone with Milne's fluent pen. The manuscript of *Winnie-the-Pooh* does not really show how few changes he made because it was his practice to make a pencil draft, which was thrown away, before the surviving ink manuscript, but there is no doubt that he did write quickly and fluently, that the stories came easily. Eeyore, Piglet and, of course, Pooh, the toys already in the nursery, were at the heart of the book. He had invented Owl and Rabbit, and then he and Daphne had returned to the toy department at Harrods on a deliberate mission to acquire a new character or two. Kanga and Roo had looked the most promising candidates and duly inspired the seventh story. By March *Winnie-the-Pooh* was largely written.

None of the stories in *The Secret* were written after the date of the list. The proofs of *Four Plays* were swiftly returned, in time for Chatto and Windus to publish on

15 April. There was no hurry about the *Saki* introduction or the further children's poems, and he remained reluctant to write a pantomime for Playfair.

So it is no wonder that he had plenty of time to involve himself in the whole business of the illustration, design, layout, production and the finances of *Winnie-the-Pooh*. 'Milne's instructions were detailed, far more so than any Kipper had received from other authors,' said Rawle Knox. 'Kipper' was Shepard's nickname, but Milne never used it. They were still not at all close. 'I always had to start again at the beginning with Milne every time I met him, I think he retired into himself – very often and for long periods,' Shepard said much later, but the letters suggest Milne was not at all withdrawn at this point. He often pressed Shepard for meetings.

Shepard had always worked from models – 'The idea of working without models never occurred to him.' Milne knew this and was anxious, in March 1926, that the artist should come to Mallord Street and meet the toys. 'I think you must come here on Thursday, if only to get Pooh's and Piglet's likeness.' But he wanted Piglet small 'as you will see when you read the sixth story' – that is the one where Piglet is too small to reach the knocker. In the original sketch, in the *Royal Magazine*,

Piglet is shown in mid-air, jumping up and down. For the book, Shepard provided a convenient flowerpot. In fact, it was even more important that Piglet should be small for the seventh story – the rather disquieting story where Kanga and Roo are not welcomed to the Forest, and Piglet impersonates the kidnapped joey and jumps into Kanga's pocket in his place. 'It is hard to be brave when you're only a Very Small Animal,' says Piglet, and Rabbit responds, 'It is because you are a very small animal that you will be Useful in the adventure before us.'

From the beginning the appearance of the toys had shaped their characters. Milne himself had said that you could see at once that Eeyore was gloomy and Piglet squeaky. 'As for Pooh', Milne wrote (sending four of the stories 'so that you can get an idea of them at once'): 'I want you to see Billy's Bear. He has such a nice expression.' But Shepard had been drawing teddy bears for years, based on his son Graham's Growler, that magnificent bear, and he was really not inclined to change now. Growler was there already, anyway, in *When We Were Very Young*, not only as himself in 'Teddy Bear', but clearly identified as Christopher Robin's own bear, on his bed in the last picture in the book.

Shepard would even go so far as to say (after Milne's

death and, indeed, after the death of his own son) that he used Graham as the model for the child: 'Christopher Robin's legs were too skinny. So I decided to draw my own son, Graham, who was a sturdy little boy. Otherwise I was a stickler for accuracy. All the illustrations of Christopher Robin and Pooh and Piglet and the other animals were drawn exactly where Milne had visualised them – usually in Ashdown Forest.' It was a natural enough claim for Shepard to make in his extreme old age. But Graham was eighteen at the time of *Winnie-the-Pooh*, and indeed anyone who has seen the juxtaposition in Christopher Milne's own memoirs of the 'butterfly photo' and one of Shepard's drawings would find it difficult to give much credence to Shepard's claim. Christopher's real legs look quite as sturdy as in the drawings, and Christopher himself would say, 'It is true that he used his imagination when he drew the animals but me he drew from life. I did indeed look just like that.' The clothes, the hairstyle – that was just how they were, his mother's ideas carried out by Nanny, who made the smocks and shorts and cut (rather rarely) his hair.

John Macrae of Dutton's, Milne's American publisher, claimed to have been in the room, presumably in March 1926, when the partnership was in action.

During the process of bringing Winnie-the-Pooh into existence, I happened to be present at one of the meetings of Milne and Shepard – Milne sitting on the sofa reading the story, Christopher Robin sitting on the floor playing with the characters, which are now famous in *Winnie-the-Pooh*, and, by his side, on the floor, sat E. H. Shepard making sketches for the illustrations which finally went into the book ... Christopher Robin, the true inspiration of these four books to both the author and the artist, was entirely unconscious of his part in the drama.

This sounds a little too neat, a little too good to be true, but it is accurate enough to what we know (Shepard did sketch the animals in pencil from what Milne called 'the living model') and was written only nine years after the event.

Milne's own view of his American publisher was rather more astringent. 'He is an old man with a beard, and he calls me "Sir" all the time. Not "Yes, sir" *à la Americaine*, but "Yessir", like a Boy Scout. Very trying. He is always bowing to me, and telling me how I go straight to the hearts of the people.' After all, there had never been anything quite like *When We Were Very Young*. 'I also go straight to the heart of his banker, I should imagine,' Milne wrote to Ken.

In the spring of 1926 Shepard was having to work against the clock, as the *Royal Magazine* had taken six of the stories, needed to go to press, according to Milne, 'months in advance' and was naturally anxious all the stories would appear before the book was published in October. At one stage, Miss Pearn, in the magazine department at Curtis Brown, wrote to Milne, 'Will you be so kind as to pass this S.O.S. on to Mr Shepard', and three days later wrote to Shepard to say, 'Mr Milne has asked us to communicate direct with you in future in connection with the *Winnie-the-Pooh* drawings.' In April, Shepard was in Rapallo and the *Royal Magazine* was getting a bit nervous about timing. 'I am relieved to hear that you are now at work,' Miss Pearn wrote.

Milne seemed to be acting as a financial middleman, as well as being closely concerned in the content of the illustrations. 'They were going to pay you £12.10 a story' (that was for one large and four to six small drawings). 'I have told C.B. to try and raise them, as I didn't think you would be satisfied with this; but in a way it is all extra, and I hope we shall get much more from America. The trouble is there is so little time.'

Dutton's were very anxious to get the original two – Bees and Rabbit – out as soon as possible for their salesmen to take round to the bookshops. Frederick

Muller at Methuen agreed to get those two stories (which had already appeared in the *Evening News* and *Eve*) 'set up in galley proof ... then we had all three better meet and try to arrange the make-up of it' – that is Muller, Milne, Shepard. At the *Royal Magazine* they were making up the pages for their first story, actually the fourth in the book, called at that stage: 'Winnie-the-Pooh finds a Tail'. In the magazine it was squashed into only four and a half pages, with Shepard providing thirteen pictures altogether, including nine of Eeyore in various odd positions – rather than the six or seven Milne had suggested would be called for. In the book itself, 'In which Eeyore loses a tail and Pooh finds one' takes up twelve pages. On 24 March, Daphne was able to write to Shepard (as A. A. Milne *pp* D. M. – having abandoned a fictitious 'Celia Brice', at least as far as Shepard was concerned) to tell him that 'the *Royal* has gone up to 15 guineas'.

It was Milne's idea that Shepard should have a share of his royalties this time, recognising his permanent share in the books. It was extremely unusual for an illustrator at this period. The agreed proportion seems to have been Milne's own suggestion. The contracts remained primarily between Milne and the publishers, with subsidiary agreements made between Milne and Shepard. The contract for *Winnie-the-Pooh*, signed on 15 March 1926, said 'that the publishers agree to publish the said work with illustrations by E. H. Shepard, to be provided by the author without cost to the publishers'. The contract for *When We Were Very Young* (10 April 1924) had said the publishers agreed the book should be 'suitably illustrated at their own expense'. The two further children's books would follow the pattern for *Pooh* – and when the rights to reproduce Shepard's drawings as toys, wallpaper and so on were granted in both England and America, again it was 'by agreement with the author'. The characters, both Christopher Robin and the toys themselves, adapted by Shepard from the reality, and Owl and Rabbit imagined by Shepard from Milne's invention, were never, in any sense, Shepard's property. Milne wrote to Shepard:

> *Brown has drawn up the agreements with Dutton and Methuen for* Winnie-the-Pooh. *In them you get £200 on account from M. and £100 from D. (less commission) – i.e. you get £270 anyway, if not a single copy is sold. Which is better than* When We Were Very Young, *for, I should imagine, fewer drawings. As regards royalties Dutton and Methuen were prepared to pay 20% and 25% (i.e. 4% and 5% for you) but protested*

that it wouldn't leave them much margin for
advertisement. So now D. pays 15% to 5,000, and
then 20%, and Methuen pays 20% to 10,000,
22½% to 15,000 and then 25%. If it is the success
we hope and expect it to be, we ought to do at least
50,000 in England and 100,000 in America – in
fact there is really no limit to what we might do,
and the sales will go on for a long time.

A little later, when presumably the advance had been
increased, Milne wrote to Ken:

Shepard and I are having a joint agreement,
dividing in the proportion of 80 to 20. Actually he
did all the WWWVY illustrations for £200, and as
on this book we are getting £1,000 in advance
from England and £1,000 from America, he gets
£400 straight off. And, of course, should eventually
get much more. But when I told Daff of the
suggested division, 80% to me, 20% to him, she said,
'I am sure you make it sound all right to him, but it
will want a lot of explaining to Mrs Shepard.'

The two women had met when the whole Shepard family
went down to Cotchford for the day to give the artist a

chance to sketch and explore the actual setting of the book, 'all the spots where the things happened'. If Milne seemed reticent and rather stiff in Mallord Street, it was not so in Sussex that spring. 'He was a different man,' Shepard remembered many years later. 'He was quite different, going over the ground and showing me the places.' Milne had, in fact, had only just a year to get to know Ashdown Forest, but he already loved it, and as he wrote the stories, though the landscape is hardly mentioned, they are set firmly in a real place under a real sky.

Another good writer, Barbara Willard, who lived on the edge of the Forest and had used the place in her own books, said to me that the Pooh books, 'could just as well have been set on Hampstead Heath', but the stories have a much more rural feeling than that suggests and the illustrations are still recognisably of the Sussex background Milne showed to Shepard more than ninety years ago. The October 1987 hurricane did terrible damage in the Forest and devastated the wood the Milnes planted in the field along the lane from their house – but Gills Lap is still recognisable as 'the enchanted place on the very top of the Forest'. New pines have grown to replace those that fell and there is now some undergrowth and not quite so much of the 'close-set grass, quiet and smooth and green', where you can sit down carelessly like Pooh.

Milne and Shepard walked up to Gills Lap across open country that is more heathland than forest, over dry golden grass, between bent dead bracken (with no sign yet of the new season's growth), tangled gorse and heather. They saw, as Pooh and Christopher Robin did, 'the whole world spread out until it reached the sky'. Now, in a secluded spot, a 'warm and sunny spot', if it's that sort of day, you can find, if you look hard enough, a memorial to the two men, writer and artist.

On that spring day they walked down the hill to the river in the valley and saw under the trees in Posingford Wood clumps of yellow primroses, sheets of white anemones ('like driven snow against the trees'), patches of bluebells and the buds of marsh marigolds just beginning to show a little gold. They crossed the wooden bridge and returned along the lane in time for tea. Mary, Shepard's daughter, would remember Christopher Robin's delight when her big brother, Graham (soon to go up to Oxford), played with the child in the stream, 'with an old log floating there that became a battleship, an alligator.' She thought Christopher Robin reacted as one who had never known 'anyone older than himself actually playing games with him'. In fact, the only child spent a good deal of time playing what he called 'dog games' with his father – running after balls, hitting balls, catching balls – but there were also messier, less structured games: scooping mud and scum and weed from the stream, looking for lost golf balls, and landing instead grass snakes and nobbly newts. He had a number of companions nearer his own age too – Anne Darlington, when she was visiting, as she did very often; Brenda Tasker, the gardener's daughter, who would remember building huts out of bracken, playing cricket and riding Jessica, the donkey; and Hannah, who lived only half a mile away, and was good at climbing trees. It was in the apple orchard up the lane – full of excellent trees for climbing – that Roo was lost and never found again. Olive Brockwell remembered the heartache of that search all her life.

Part of the strength and charm of the stories comes from the juxtaposition of toy animal and forest. Milne writes something simple, such as Pooh was 'walking through the forest one day, humming proudly to himself', and Shepard shows a jaunty toy bear walking through real Ashdown Forest over real rough grass with real trees in the background; or Milne writes: 'One fine winter's day when Piglet was brushing away the snow in front of his house', and Shepard shows a diminutive toy piglet making a tiny path with a tiny broom away from the trunk of a fine beech tree. Trees dominate the books. Rabbit lives in a burrow, which has some relationship to Badger's house in the middle of the Wild Wood (but there are no stoats and weasels, no cudgels or pistols in Milne's forest); nearly everyone else lives in trees, including Christopher Robin himself.

It had all started in a tree in the garden at Cotchford – an ancient walnut tree (now long gone). 'The tree was hollow inside and a great gash in its trunk had opened up to make a door.' It was the perfect tree-house for a five-year-old. 'There was plenty of room for a boy and his bear.' They could sit on the soft crumbly floor and see, high above them, 'a green and blue ceiling of leaves and sky'. And even if Nanny could hear him if he called, it was a sort of independence and he was getting more adventurous every day. Christopher would recall: 'So if anyone wonders why in the stories so much time seems to be spent in trees or up trees, the answer is that this, in real life, was how it was.' Milne wrote in 1927, just after Christopher's seventh birthday: 'At the moment he is mad on tree-climbing, which he really does rather well and pluckily, even after doing the last eight feet (downwards) on his head the other day.' This is the sort of boy behind the stories, not the long-ago kneeling child with the little gold head.

There have been critics who have found Christopher Robin, even in the *Pooh* books, a stumbling block to their full enjoyment. 'Was there ever a more insufferable child than Christopher Robin?' wrote the critic Chris Powling on the sixtieth birthday of the book. Like Geoffrey Grigson on the poems, again he seems to let sociology and class-consciousness get in the way:

> Every inch of him exudes smugness – from the top of that curious, bobbed haircut to the tip of those tiny-tot sandals (and the smock and shorts in between are just as irritating). Okay, so we shouldn't take him at face value. Maybe there is deep irony in this twentieth-century version of the Victorian Beautiful Child. In Christopher Robin's case, however, we must certainly heed the wise advice of Oscar Wilde that it's only a superficial person who does not judge by appearances. With Milne's prose [his 'sheer literary craftsmanship'] reinforced by E. H. Shepard's superb line-drawings, Christopher Robin must surely be what he seems. And what he seems is a serious affront to anyone who believes children are simply people who haven't lived very long.

Powling, in fact, comes round to knowing that the stories can survive even the 'insufferable' too-perfect child:

The permanence of the *Pooh* books has nothing whatever to do with their psychological depth or the sharpness of their social comment or their status as morality. These don't matter a jot. What's important, through and through, is their success as storytelling. And this is a triumph. It survives shifts in fashion. It survives Christopher Robin. It even survives that odd tone-of-voice which, for all Milne's simple language, never quite settles for a child audience. The world Pooh creates is completely unique and utterly self-sustaining. Yes, it is a world that's very like ours . . . but much, much more like itself.

That phrase 'the world Pooh creates' seems at first like a slip. Didn't he really mean to say 'the world Milne creates' or 'the world of Pooh . . .'? In fact, it gives us the clue why Christopher Robin is the way he is – too perfect, flawless, not falling out of trees. It is because he is seen in relation to Pooh and the other animals. Pooh and Piglet are the children and the boy himself takes on the role of the adult. The listening or reading child identifies with the superior strength and power he sometimes resents in the adults around him, however much he loves his parents. Christopher Robin is always resourceful and competent; he is the child as hero. In 'the world Pooh creates' it is Christopher

Robin who reads sustaining books at moments of crisis, who comes to the rescue, who will make sure that no harm comes to the kidnapped Roo (whatever befell him in real life) and protects the animals from the teeth of fierce things. ('If Christopher Robin is coming, I don't mind anything.') He dries Eeyore's tail after its immersion in the river (having nailed it on on a previous occasion) and does all the comforting and useful things that parents do. The boy is brave and godlike to the toys, just as the loving parent is to a small child. It is absolutely beside the point to criticise him for being too good to be true.

Just occasionally, as any adult does too, Christopher Robin reveals his frailty, his feet of clay, and this surely adds to his appeal. He has forgotten what the North Pole looks like. ('I did know once . . .') It is Pooh who is childlike, egotistical, hungry, alternately boastful and self-deprecating, occasionally managing to be brave and unselfish, accepting things without really understanding them, as children so often have to accept un-understandable explanations. The listening or reading child recognises himself in Pooh and recognises himself as he longs to be, as he thinks he will be, in Christopher Robin. He recognises and enjoys the wit and tenderness of the books.

But after *The Pooh Perplex*, Frederick Crews' 1963 parody of a student casebook, one cannot attempt the most rudimentary criticism without seeming to be joking. After 'The Hierarchy of Heroism in *Winnie-the-Pooh*' and '*A la recherche du Pooh perdu*' (Weltschmerz, alienation and the rest) one's pen freezes in one's hand. Perhaps, with all that chasing after honey, the books explore the universality of the sexual urge or the bestiality of the free market? Perhaps the great Heffalump expedition really is a paradigm of colonialism? Eeyore is certainly the archetypal outsider, if not the spokesman for the disillusioned postwar generation of the 1920s. 'There is something a little frightening about *The Pooh Perplex*', as Benedict Nightingale wrote in a review. You begin to wonder if those invented critics may not have something after all, underneath their ludicrous jargon.

As Alison Lurie put it, Crews managed 'to stifle almost all critical comment on Winnie-the-Pooh for a decade'. She felt she was, in 1972, merely following up one of the suggestions made by 'Smedley Force', a prominent member of the Modern Language Association of America, who was struck by 'the paucity of biographical connections between *Winnie-the-Pooh* and the lives of A. A. Milne, "Christopher Robin", and the historical personages who probably lie behind the fictional portraits of "Pooh", "Piglet", "Kanga" et alia.' Lurie makes the suggestion that Pooh's relation to Piglet is much like that of Milne's older brother, Ken, to Milne himself. She sees something of J. V. Milne in Owl and something of Milne's mother Maria in, not Kanga, but Rabbit. She points out, as many others have done, that we all know people like Tigger, like Eeyore, like Kanga. Humphrey Carpenter suggests, 'Don't we, indeed, recognise them in ourselves?' He saw that Milne makes it possible for a child 'to carry into adult life a perception of human character acquired from his readings' of the *Pooh* books. If Milne sets out to depict only a very small fraction of human behaviour, 'he manages to do so completely within a child's understanding; the *Pooh* books can be taken in fully by all but the smallest children.' And yet the adult reading aloud is not bored. It is an extraordinary achievement.

Richard Adams has suggested that Eeyore is 'the first portrait in English literature of a type of neurotic we all know only too well' – though he may owe a little to Dickens's poor Mrs Gummidge in *David Copperfield*, 'the lone lorn creetur', who did not appear to be able to cheer up, drowned in self-pity as she was. 'My trouble has made me contrary,' she said, and Eeyore's troubles make him contrary too, but Milne makes self-pity far funnier and more lovable. Eeyore has moments of happiness which save him from being a caricature – for instance, when his tail is restored and when he puts his burst birthday balloon into his useful pot. Adams says it was from the *Pooh* books that he learnt for *Watership Down* (one of the few comparable bestsellers, at least in the initial years) 'the vital importance, as protagonists, of a group of clearly portrayed, contrasting but reciprocal characters', though he does not claim that his rabbits come anywhere near Pooh and his friends.

There have been many different reasons given for the enduring appeal of the books. It has been suggested it is because they are stories of 'universal perplexity', that we are all bears of very little brain trying as Pooh does to bluff our way through life. 'Hardly anybody knows if those are these or these are those.' And as Pooh can be a brave and clever bear, we feel we could be too, if only life would give us the chance. If the critic John Rowe Townsend, realising 'how very good they are', considers the stories 'as totally without hidden significance as anything ever written', another critic, Peter Hunt, responds by saying that they are 'still the complex work of a complex man, and they include a fascinating series of subtexts that can tell us a lot about the relationships of child, adult, story and book.' It is 'sophisticated writing, the pace, the timing, and the narrative stance all contributing to the comic effect'.

Alison Lurie suggests it is because Milne 'created out of a few acres of Sussex countryside, a world that has the qualities both of the Golden Age of history and legend, and the lost paradise of childhood – two eras which, according to psychologists, are often one in the unconscious mind'. The small adventures are concerned entirely with the things children are most interested in – friends, food, birthdays, tree-houses and expeditions, jokes and songs. They are concerned, as children are, with courage that comes and goes. There is no economic necessity or competition. The dangers are all natural ones – bees, heffalumps (possibly), bad weather – and what is celebrated is community, the spirit of co-operation and kindness, most clearly seen in *Winnie-the-Pooh* when Christopher Robin and Pooh rescue Piglet when he is entirely surrounded by water.

Humphrey Carpenter has pointed out that Milne's humour is that of a mathematician. 'Each humorous situation in the Pooh books is reached by the logical pursuit of an idea to the point of absurdity.' Milne's pleasure is in playing with words. Carpenter suggests he 'handles words in the kind of detached manner in which a mathematician deals with figures' but, in fact, there is plenty of emotion in the Forest. If Christopher Robin is godlike, he is certainly the god of love. The feminist critic, Carol Stanger, sees that the stories appeal because 'they respect what is traditionally given low status in patriarchal society, nurturing and emotion'. They reflect a pre-sexual, pre-literate world that is kinder and more attractive than the world as it is; and even critics who say – like Roger Sale and Margery Fisher – that they can no longer enjoy the stories as much as they did as children, or as much as college students often do today, none the less find themselves still moved by the thought of their own vanished *Pooh*-reading childhoods.

In July, three months before the book was published, someone was already after the manuscript. Milne wrote to E. V. Lucas: 'If I give a price now, I say £350. If the book is a complete failure, this may be reduced to 2/9; on the other hand, it may go up to £500 ... I wouldn't give £350 for anybody's manuscript ... But I don't want to make the mistake I made with the verse.' In fact, he never did sell the manuscripts of *Winnie-the-Pooh* or its sequel, and in his will instructed his trustees, after the death of his wife, to offer the two manuscripts to the library of his old college, Trinity, Cambridge, as a gift. And that is where they are now.

Winnie-the-Pooh was dedicated to Daphne in one of those almost embarrassingly open gestures which seem so strange from a man whose son would say, 'My father's heart remained buttoned up all through his life'.

TO HER

HAND IN HAND WE COME
CHRISTOPHER ROBIN AND I
TO LAY THIS BOOK IN YOUR LAP.
SAY YOU'RE SURPRISED?
SAY YOU LIKE IT?
SAY IT'S JUST WHAT YOU WANTED?
BECAUSE IT'S YOURS—
BECAUSE WE LOVE YOU.

Here it seems that Alan Milne is wearing his heart on his sleeve – a necessary gesture, perhaps, when the child's mother has been so totally excluded from both the books for children. Nanny was in the first, *When We Were Very Young*, over and over again, and so was Milne himself – Shepard actually drew him (with cap and pipe) in 'Sand-between-the-toes'. All Daphne got was 'God bless Mummy' and a possible (undesirable) association with the disappearing mother of James James Morrison

Morrison. Long afterwards, Ronald Bryden in the *Spectator* looked at the poems and decided that whether the mother's absences 'betoken drink, drugs, insanity or infidelity, the child has obviously been driven by some emotional deprivation into a life of lonely fantasy, inventing a series of imaginary playmates': Binker, mice, beetles, even raindrops – quite apart from the toys themselves. The mother has surely failed in her role. Now in *Pooh* the conversations between the boy and his father make the framework of the book, and there is no room at all for the mother.

Ernest Shepard's copy of the book would later carry Milne's inscription:

> *When I am gone,*
> *Let Shepard decorate my tomb,*
> *And put (if there is room)*
> *Two pictures on the stone:*
> *Piglet, from page a hundred and eleven*
> *And Pooh and Piglet walking (157) . . .*
> *And Peter, thinking that they are my own,*
> *Will welcome me to heaven.*

That is Piglet 'blowing happily at a dandelion and wondering whether it would be this year, next year, some time or never', whatever 'it' was; and Pooh and Piglet (Pooh clasping his special pencil case, so like Christopher Robin's real one) walking thoughtfully home together in the golden evening, at the very end of the book. This gives us moving evidence of how much Alan Milne admired Ernest Shepard's contribution to the books.

In the spring of 1926 the *Evening News* had carried an article by Milne, lamenting the attitude to writers of the British Broadcasting Company, formed three and a half years before. Milne wrote to Ken, sending him his play *The Ivory Door* to read:

> I also send the Evening News: *sorry you don't read it, nor live in London where the whole metropolis is placarded on these occasions with my name, practically life-size. On second thoughts, I think perhaps you're lucky . . . I called it 'Authors and the B.B.C. by an author' and asked for 10 guineas, to which they said promptly '15, if you sign it'. Did I hesitate? Not for a moment.*

It seems worth giving most of the article here for, if the BBC has, in over ninety years, improved its attitude and payments, the general feeling about writers seems to have stayed much the same. Not long ago, for example, Philip

Pullman initiated a campaign in Oxford pressing literary festivals not to expect writers to take part without proper payment.

Complaint was made in the *Evening News* a few days ago that the programmes of the B.B.C. were of a much lower standard on the literary side than on the musical side. I should like to suggest, from the author's point of view, some reasons why this is so.

Authors have never been taken very seriously by their fellow-men. 'A singer is a singer,' the attitude seems to be, 'a painter is a painter, and a sculptor sculpts; but, dash it all, a writer only writes, which is a thing we all do every day of our lives, and the only difference between ourselves and Thomas Hardy is that Hardy doesn't do anything else, whereas we are busy men with a job of real work to do.' And since writing is, in a sense, the hobby, or at least the spare-time occupation of the whole world, it has become natural for the layman to regard the professional author as also engaged merely upon a hobby . . .

Now the B.B.C. exploits to its highest power this attitude of kindly condescension to the author. To the B.B.C. all authors are the same author. There is a 'regular fee' for the author, whoever he is; the fee is what advertisers call 'nominal'; and with any luck the B.B.C. can avoid paying even this ridiculous amount by an ingenious scheme of its own. It says to the author: 'If we pay you a fee, we won't mention your name or your works or your publishers or anything about you, but if you will let us do it for nothing we will announce to our thousand million book-buying listeners where your work is to be bought. And if you don't like it, you can leave it, because there are plenty of other authors about; and, if it came to the worst, we could write the things ourselves quite easily . . .'

But the B.B.C. is obsessed by the thought of advertisement. Publicity might never have been heard of until the B.B.C. was born. After all, if the B.B.C. says to the author, 'I shan't pay you, because I'm helping your books to sell,' why on earth shouldn't the publisher also say to the author, 'And I shan't pay you, because I'm helping you to get taken up by the B.B.C.'? Why should the Broadcasting Company be the one, and the only one, not to pay?

I suggest, then, that the reason why the literary standard of the B.B.C. is low is simply that the Company has made no effort to attract authors, and is entirely out of touch and sympathy with authors. Let me give an example or two from my own experience.

1) I was offered two guineas to read one act of one of my own plays. Whether this was an attractive proposition for listeners-in is not for me to say, but how could anyone think that it was an attractive proposition for the author? Let anybody consider what, in the way of preparation and performance, the author would have to go through, and ask himself if the offer was likely to be accepted.

2) On a very special 'Gala Night' I was asked to read something of my own during the Children's Hour. I was offered five guineas, and it was explained to me apologetically that the Children's Hour had to be run cheaply. (As if that was any reason why I should help the B.B.C. to run it cheaply!) I replied that I didn't want to read my work aloud. An Editor, a Manager, a Publisher, would then automatically have said, 'Would you do it for ten guineas?' or 'What would you do it for?' – or something of that sort. The B.B.C. voice at the other end of the telephone said in heart-rending accents, 'Not even for the sake of the Little Ones?'

3) I was asked, in common with, I think, every known dramatist from the highest downwards,

if I would write an original one act play for the Company. I said that, apart from anything else, it would be impossible for the B.B.C. to pay a fee at all comparable with the royalties one might expect from a stage-play, and that, in this case, such a fee would be necessary, seeing that there were no subsidiary stage-rights to be got from a play specially written for listeners only; I was told proudly in reply that, indeed and on the contrary whatever, they were prepared to pay as much as fifty pounds . . . !

4) And finally a letter from America; for indeed the Broadcasting Manner knows no frontiers. But in this case there is a difference. An author, to the American B.C., is, at any rate, an individual. In a letter to my agent the A.B.C. says lyrical things about me, such as the B.B.C. never felt about any author. Why can't they broadcast my plays – those lovely, adorable things? What can they do to persuade me? Are tears, prayers, quotations from Ella Wheeler Wilcox, letters of introduction from the President, alike useless? 'What is the next step we can take? What is there I should do?' It is a cry from the heart.

And then, suddenly an inspiration occurs to him. Can it be? Absurd! Still – you never know. Just worth trying, perhaps. So he tries,

'Is it a question of royalty? You have but to say the word if that is what is holding him back?'

Yes, it was. Fancy! An author wanting money, just as if he were a real worker! What on earth does the fellow do for it?

Milne was much in demand. A film producer telephoned to ask if he could come and film the author at work: 'Entering the Library after Kissing Wife Farewell – Deep in Thought – Interrupted by Prattling Child – Takes Child on Knee and Pats Head of Same – Sudden Inspiration – Throws Child Away and Seizes Pen – Writes – Fade Out.' Milne said he did not think it was much of an idea, whereupon the producer, almost like the B.B.C., brought up the educational effect, if not on the Little Ones, then certainly on the Lower Classes. The producer then brought out his most compelling argument: 'In fact, Mr Milne, I assure you that I would sooner – you will hardly credit this but it is true – I would sooner film a really great artistic genius than an Earl.' To clinch the matter he then added that he had already got Gilbert Frankau. And Milne rang off.

Milne also refused the blandishments of an envoy of

Pears' Soap. They had had a tremendous success years earlier when they had bought Sir John Millais' Academy painting *Bubbles* and, inserting a cake of soap into it, had created the most widely known advertisement in the world. Now they wanted Milne to follow his contribution to the previous year's Christmas *Annual* with a story actually tailor-made to their product. They had wined and dined him in a private room in the Ritz with the other distinguished contributors to the *Annual* (E. V. Lucas and Heath Robinson among them). Might not this have softened him up for what they really wanted – a children's story about soap bubbles? Clara Hawkins, who had edited the *Annual*, recorded her visit to Mallord Street, which she apparently thought to be a great deal older than it really was:

A. A. Milne lives in Chelsea, and there I went upon appointment. The houses of Chelsea are old and gracious of manner; with the classic red brick and white paint austerity of their Georgian origin relieved by brilliant doors of primary reds or blues or yellows – the happy inspiration of their present day bohemian owners. Mr Milne's doorway was a brilliant blue. There was a little stoop in front of it where I stood for one moment to catch my breath. I rang. A maid admitted me and led me into a grey, orange-curtained little room that was austere and cold. I was glad I had an appointment. This little room had an atmosphere forbidding to autograph hunters or timid maiden writers seeking comfort.

At last the maid returned and led me down a little hallway to a room at the end, the door of which she opened, at the same time announcing 'Miss Hawkins'. Inside the room there was a bluish haze of nice-smelling pipe smoke, and inside the smoke there was a lean, pleasant young man. He got up lazily as if he were a little tired after a long tramp on the moors. That was my impression of him – tweeds, dogs, gorse, and a pipe. As a matter of fact I don't believe he is especially any of these things; I just thought of them as he stood up to shake my hand. [Later he said] 'Are you interested in houses?'

I answered, 'I have been envying you this one ever since you have been talking to me.'

He looked pleased and said, 'It really is a nice one isn't it? Would you like to see it? It's rather a hobby of my wife's and mine.'

I followed him up the stairs, little winding stairs that led a charming way up to the second floor. He opened a door and out came a shower of golden light. We entered the drawing-room. It was a perfect little room, with Georgian panels and original cornices and a fire-place in the manner of William Kent. The whole of it had been painted a brilliant glowing yellow, with the mouldings picked out in gold. On the walls, in the centre of each panel, there were pictures that were great blobs of red and yellow and orange done in the modern manner and extraordinarily effective. The room was a burning sun in the middle of grey and sober London! Milne looked at me and I nodded my head.

'You like it?' he said. 'Now come and see my wife's room.'

Down a narrow passage we went, through a door, and again gold flooded out upon us. Only gold this time with a glowing rose-colour mellowing it. There was a great Italian four-poster, painted Italian chairs. It was a curious combination of modernity and ancient grace, very well done.

'My wife rather goes in for this sort of thing,' he said. We returned to his study.

'You're an American,' he said. 'Of course you must be, else you wouldn't have been so interested in my house.' And then abruptly he turned to me:

'You want me to write about soap bubbles, do you, as an advertisement?'

'For children, Mr Milne,' I said pleadingly.

But Milne was not to be persuaded – 'not even for the sake of the Little Ones'. No money was mentioned, and Miss Hawkins had to be content with the promise of another contribution to *Pears' Annual*. She left 'glowing because he was so nice. I had absolutely forgotten that he hadn't done a thing I'd asked him to do.'

Milne was also approached by the makers of Wolsey children's underwear. 'The story would of course be left entirely to Mr Milne, subject only to there being included in it some, so to speak, fatherly remarks upon the warmth and wisdom of children being under-clothed in wool.' But Milne was no more inclined to promote underwear than soap.

Christopher Robin had made a fleeting appearance during Miss Hawkins's visit – sucking his thumb and sitting on the stairs. Miss Hawkins had seen him as the three-year-old she had wanted to see, but in fact he was a schoolboy now. He had started at Miss Walters' School in Tite Street, in Chelsea. He went with Anne Darlington and the daughters of another neighbour, who had also become a friend – Denis Mackail, grandson of Burne-Jones, brother of Angela Thirkell, whose mother's first cousins included Stanley Baldwin and Rudyard Kipling. Milne had written to him after *Greenery Street* – they had met before the war, in J. M. Barrie's cricket team – and Milne had found him decidedly interesting as a person, with his 'special fits of depression', his 'special brand of nightmares' and his occasional 'flickers of sunshine', as he tried to support with his pen an extravagant household in another Chelsea house. They had a lot of friends in common – not only Barrie (Mackail would write his first biography), but P. G. Wodehouse, Ian Hay, the Darlingtons. The new friendship survived a disastrous first lunch party. Mackail wrote:

> It was as near a complete failure as anything could well be. I was desperately shy, but so was my host. Moreover the Milnes had a refectory table in those days, which when four people are seated at it means that two are much too close together, while the other two are much too far apart. Yet though I should like to blame the table entirely, I know that I was dull and tongue-tied and that Alan ... must bitterly have regretted ever having posted his letter.

Later they would laugh at that first occasion as they dined with each other over and over again. (There was one particularly memorable evening in November 1927 when a taxi went through a wall on the other side of the road and no one heard it because they were all listening to Barrie – 'There was always considerable anxiety before-hand as to whether he were going to lift the whole party to glorious heights or plunge it into silence and gloom.') Milnes and Mackails went to theatres together ('Every outing concluded by our being deposited, in their bright blue car, at our own front door'), visited each other's country cottages in the summers and each other's children's parties at Christmas. Mary was a year older than Christopher Robin and Anne was two years younger than both Christopher and Anne Darlington. The Milne children's party was always an outing to the theatre, combined with some sort of splendid meal. Milne and Wodehouse together put Mackail up for the Garrick and, though Wodehouse resigned almost immediately after-wards ('I loathe clubs . . . I hated the Garrick more than any of them'), Mackail would often go in Milne's car for lunch in Garrick Street.

Milne described the Tite Street school in a letter to Ken in June 1926:

> *Billy loves his school, though I never quite know*
> *what he is doing. He brings home weird works of*
> *art from time to time, hand-painted pottery and*
> *what not, which has to be disposed of by Daff. They*
> *also teach him to catch. (This is really rather a good*

school.) Yesterday he bounced the ball on the ground
and caught it with the right hand 20 times
running, thus earning a penny from his gratified
papa. He says he's done 10 times with the left hand,
but not visibly.

The boy was also giving some thought to the future. One afternoon when Daphne and Nanny were both out, father and son had some serious talk on their own. 'Do parents and children understand each other better than they did?' an interviewer would ask A. A. Milne, who replied: 'I think they try more and they certainly should . . . But there is still a kind of shyness between the child and the parent.' On this occasion Milne told his son that when he was about ten he would go to a boarding school. The boy said, a little wistfully, 'Do I ever come back to you after that?' They talked about careers too, and after the boy had rejected various suggestions the idea of elephant hunting came up. 'As long as I wasn't eaten,' he said, and then, after a moment's thought, 'Or trodden on.' ('I can't bear to think of him being trodden on by an elephant,' Milne wrote to Ken.) When he was grown up, Christopher said that he had never told anybody that it was an elephant, a real live elephant, that he had most wanted. What he had at Cotchford (on a count in 1927, when he was seven) were 'two bantams, two rabbits, several kittens, six snails, a lot of caterpillars and a horrible collection of beetles'.

Milne also reported a walk when he was beginning to get irritated because his son was continually lagging behind:

> ME: *Come on, Moon.*
>
> MOON: *I'm just looking at something, Blue. [That was what Christopher normally called his father, as did many other people.]*
>
> ME: *(rather impatiently): Oh, do come on!*
>
> MOON: *(running up, terribly respectfully): Yes, father. Yes, father. Yes, father!*
>
> *Which makes all parental sternness simply impossible.*

Milne once said that he thought it impossible for anyone with a sense of humour to be a good father. 'The necessary assumption of authority and wisdom seems so ridiculous.' 'It is the old conflict of duty and affection, and correction is still a difficulty . . . Over and over again you hear the threat "If you do that again I'll punish you . . ." and, if he does it again, how can we help admiring his pluck, seeing how small he is and how big we are.'

Christopher, when adult, would have some interesting things to say about this; he thought that his father 'had inherited some of his own father's gifts as a teacher', but that he could never have been one himself. 'He could radiate enthusiasm, but he could never impose discipline.' His 'relationships were always between equals, however old or young, distinguished or undistinguished the other person'. Christopher remembered how, at about this time, his father had chided him gently for sitting at the lunch table, between mouthfuls, with his hands on the table, knife and fork pointing upwards. 'You oughtn't really to sit like that,' he said. 'Why not?' the boy asked, surprised.

'Well . . .' He hunted around for a reason he could give. Because it's considered bad manners. Because you mustn't? Because . . .

'Well', he said, looking in the direction that my fork was pointing, 'suppose somebody suddenly fell through the ceiling. They might land on your fork and that would be very painful.'

When the young Enid Blyton came to interview Milne for *Teacher's World* that October, just before the publication of *Pooh*, they naturally spoke of teachers and schools. Milne talked sympathetically of teachers who 'spend their days struggling in the poorer districts with terribly large classes'. And he couldn't resist showing off Christopher Robin's prowess with problems – exactly the same sort of problems his father had set him nearly forty years before. 'He likes problems . . . There are 500 cows in a field. They go out of a gate at the rate of two a minute. How many are left after two and a half hours?' Miss Blyton did not reveal whether the six-year-old answered that one promptly, but she did say: 'Christopher Robin finds no difficulty with problems of this sort.' A similar problem would crop up two years later in the 'Contradiction' to *The House at Pooh Corner*.

The young mathematician that day seemed to be not quite sure whether he was a dragon or a knight. He stared at Enid Blyton fiercely and blew tremendously hard. He had paper tied round his legs and she asked why. 'So's dragons won't bite me.'

He carried an enormous Teddy Bear, which he informed me was Pooh. He stood there in his little brown overall, with his great shock of corn-coloured hair, and looked about the room seeking for what he might devour. His bright eyes fell upon his father's fountain-pen and he immediately took it up and pulled it into as many pieces as possible.

This sounds destructive, but fountain pens did come apart in a rather satisfactory way and undoubtedly Christopher would have been able to put it together again, its flabby rubber tube tucked neatly away, without disgorging any ink. Christopher was already very good with his hands and would be indignant about his father's poem 'The Engineer', in *Now We Are Six*, which seems to have him saying:

> *It's a good sort of brake*
> *But it hasn't worked yet.*

'If I'd had a train (and I didn't have a train) any brake that I'd wanted to make for it – any simple thing like a brake – WOULD HAVE WORKED.'

There were numerous interviews in these years. There were numerous descriptions of the house in Mallord Street ('a rhapsody in azure and primrose' – carpets 'a heavenly blue', walls yellow) and of Milne's book-lined study – 'a neat and cosy room', looking out on 'a tiny townish garden'. Christopher would remember the smells of fuchsia and geraniums in Chelsea. There were numerous questions about how Milne liked being famous ('Well, if I am famous, then, yes, I do like it'), numerous tributes to his good looks ('his fine spare features, tanned and healthy-looking'), to his laughter, his diffidence and modesty, to his own charm, his charming wife and even more charming child.

The child was not asked at the time but he would say, much later, that 'I also quite liked being Christopher Robin and being famous. There were indeed times … when it was exciting and made me feel grand and important.' It was only later that he grew out of his part and came to resent the books so fiercely, to resent the fact that it seemed, almost, as if the father had got to where he was by climbing upon the child's own puny shoulders.

The child's grandfather said that winter: 'Alan's boy (6½), Christopher Robin, or, as he calls himself, Billy Moon, is quite unspoilt. He complains that his school is "easier than ever", but Alan thinks he learns quite enough. He makes up for it by learning chess and whist at home!' His cousin, Tony, just twelve, had been telling his grandfather that he was sure he could get a Westminster scholarship 'and is not going to be behind his father or his uncle or his brother'. When Tony's brother, Tim, had got the top scholarship to Westminster in 1925, Milne wrote to Ken: 'I only hope Billy will be as clever, but I doubt it,' and a little later added, 'I suspect him of striking out an entirely new line of his own, like Archery and

Spanish. But as long as I love him as I do now, I don't mind.'

There were a lot of hard acts for Billy Moon, alias Christopher Robin, to follow, but so far he seemed to be bearing up well. He was showing little sign of strain though he was already famous, even before *Winnie-the-Pooh* brought him further into prominence. A piece in an American magazine, *Town and Country*, in May 1926, itself raving about Milne's 'adorable nonsense' and coining the word 'Milnenomaniacs' for his fans, carried the following caption under his photograph:

A. A. Milne. English playwright. Children's poet laureate by divine right of whimsy. His plays have been successfully produced in New York. And he is the father of Christopher Robin.

Milne seemed to see no need to protect the child from all the publicity. Daphne positively encouraged the press. There is no evidence for Christopher's adult suggestion: 'I imagine that the door was guarded with extra vigilance.' Milne would say later that all the talk about Christopher Robin seemed to have nothing to do with the real child, Billy Moon. But the photographs were, of course, of the real child, whatever he was called. Milne was always allowing photographs to be taken of the two of them together. There is the famous image by Howard Coster, now in the National Portrait Gallery – Christopher Milne would say of that photograph that his father never held him like that. There are lots of other studies in less or more awkward poses. And plenty of the boy alone. Milne seemed totally confident, at least on the surface, that Christopher Robin would be able to cope when he got to prep school:

> *Years ago, school was a world of blips and buffetings, and a boy might have had a hard time, perhaps, if he had been a nursery celebrity, but conditions today are vastly different ... I am not uneasy. A delicate or lonely boy used to have a terrible time, but those days are gone, thank goodness!*

How could he have felt so sure?

In New York that spring there had been a ripple of sensation when Milton, Balch and Company published a rather clever parody of Milne and Shepard entitled *When We Were Rather Older*, focusing attention on a generation of 'modern' young things with cocktails and Charlestons and fast cars. There was some talk of a libel suit, but in fact the book (which went into a second edition immediately) did nothing but good to the original. Milne's verse was so obviously much more skilled than that of Fairfax Downey. But the book is now a collector's item itself with its own sociological interest and period charm:

> *James James*
> *Morrison's Mother's*
> *Had her hair shingled off.*
> *She's late*
> *Home for her dinner*
> *Being out shooting golf.*
> *Jim says*
> *Somebody told her*
> *That was the modern view,*
> *And since it's the rage not to be your age,*
> *Well, what can any son do?*

Milne wrote to Ken in 1926 not only of Christopher and all the interest as the Pooh stories began to appear regularly month by month in both England and America, but also of politics, of cricket and golf and of servant problems. It was the year of the General Strike, but nothing survives to tell us what Milne thought about that. The 'politics' at one point related to personalities. Apparently, Milne had sneered at Lord Bridgeman, First Lord of the Admiralty, and Ken had admonished him. In his reply to the admonition, Milne referred to an Academy painter, another old Etonian, John Collier, whose portraiture was described as achieving 'a sober veracity slightly reminiscent of Frank Holl', now hardly himself a name to conjure with. The passage seems worth quoting at length because it shows so clearly Milne's attitude to the Establishment, his inability to suffer fools gladly, which was always so characteristic of him. It also suggests Milne had a rather less conventional attitude to the avant-garde in art than some might suppose:

> *Talking of Bridgeman:*
>
> *Suppose Roger Fry (say) were to be talking of the more advanced continental painters, and were to end up: 'Meanwhile for England the shining genius of a Collier is enough' – and suppose you were to say 'Why sneer at Collier? His artistic genius is his own affair. It may not be great, but it is adequate for the work he does, work done competently and honourably' – what could Fry answer? I suppose something like this.*
>
> *'I am not "sneering" at Collier particularly; or, if I am, only in as much as he pretends to be something he isn't – that is, in as much as he gives himself the airs of a great painter. What I am really "sneering" at is the artistic perception which looks for nothing higher than a Collier,*

which is satisfied with a representative Academy full of Colliers, which tolerates the bestowal of rewards on the Colliers and the Colliers only.'

Bridgeman (from his looks, and from all I have heard of him from those who know him) is an utterly uninspired, unimaginative, rather bewildered mediocre little man, such as you could find in thousands all over England. If you say that such a man is entirely competent to fill the post of First Lord, I have no doubt you are right. But one is allowed to ask oneself: 'In that case: (1) Ought such a man to get the £5,000 a year and the honours and glory that, for some obscure reason, we have been in the habit of giving our First Lords? – and (2) Ought we to be satisfied with our methods of government, if government means nothing more than a Bridgeman rather red in the face saying "Yes. Yes" and signing something?'

Hence these sneers. The truth is that since the war I have been utterly sick of, and utterly uninterested in, politics. Perhaps the fact that I played round Ashdown Forest behind Joynson-Hicks at Easter has intensified my contempt for statesmen. My God, the profound mediocrities that emerge.

Joynson-Hicks was the Conservative Home Secretary at the time of the General Strike.

Milne went to see the MCC play the Australians and was pleased when the England team for the first test match turned out to be almost exactly the one he had predicted to Ken ('Larwood for Allen is the only difference.' He had wanted Larwood 'and he may go in yet'.) The brothers were jubilant in August when in the last match of the series a tremendous partnership between Hobbs and Sutcliffe meant the Ashes would return to England after fourteen years. 'It was a triumph for the selectors,' the papers wrote, and Milne almost felt he had been one of them.

When the family returned to London at the end of August they found that their new cook ('our Penn has left us', he had told Ken a little earlier) had been entertaining a young gentleman from Jermyn Street:

They had been living happily, honeymooning so to speak, at 13 Mallord Street, kindly borrowed from Mr and Mrs A. A. Milne. We knew nothing of this until Monday morning when we came down to breakfast and found that the cook (who had welcomed us home beamingly the afternoon before) had vanished in the night. Thereafter we heard all and more than all we wanted to. The charwoman, who comes once a week, told Daff that our house had been turned into a 'bad-ouse'; in fact from all we heard Daff and I might have been arrested for keeping one.

They returned hastily to Cotchford. Christopher did not go back to school until halfway through September. After some initial problems, they were now being very well looked after at Cotchford by a reliable couple. The handsome gardener, George Tasker (someone said he looked like a Spanish sea captain), would stay with them for the rest of his life and put up, apparently quite willingly, with Daphne's imperious ways. She was immensely pleased with the prizes they won at local horticultural shows and would introduce Tasker to visitors as her 'head gardener'. (He had a nephew who helped.) Though the Taskers lived in a cottage at the top of the drive, Tasker's daughter Brenda would remember that the only time Mrs Milne ever came there was just after the gardener's death. She came with a friend for support and Brenda could not decide 'if she was a very shy person or a complete snob, who was quite unaware of any other person around'. She had certainly been irritated many years earlier when she had to find a new cook at Cotchford because Mrs Tasker was expecting her second child, Peter.

*

Winnie-the-Pooh was published on 14 October 1926 in London and on the 21st in New York. There was one annoying misprint. Somehow Milne had left 'his' instead of 'her' for Kanga at the end of Chapter VII, having started off interestingly thinking the kangaroo a father, in spite of the pouch. (He originally wrote, 'An animal who carries his child about with him in his pocket . . .' The male pronouns are crossed out heavily in the manuscript; somehow the final 'his' in the chapter slipped through and survives in the first edition.) And some officious copy-editor had corrected Piglet's spoonerism 'spleak painly' in the same chapter: it was years before that was noticed and put right. But, in general, Milne was extremely pleased. The balance between type and illustrations was so much more satisfactory than it had been in the cluttered pages of newspapers and magazines, where the stories had made their first appearances.

The reactions to those first appearances, and the initial orders for the book, had prepared Milne for the fact that he was about to repeat the success of *When We Were Very Young* – but the reviewers could hardly believe it. The *New York Herald Tribune* said, 'As you read the conviction grows on you that Mr Milne has done it again. There are not so very many books that, sitting reading all alone, you find yourself laughing aloud over. This is one of them.

Here is nonsense in the best tradition . . . with the high seriousness about it that children and other wise people love.'

Vogue thought it was 'not quite as nice as *When We Were Very Young*, but still it has tremendous charm and is great fun to read aloud'; a St Louis paper also couldn't convince itself that the new book was quite as clever as the first one. But the great majority of the reviewers raved about it. 'Almost never has there been so much funniness in a book.' 'Mr Milne has repeated the rare coup. Once more he has written the perfect book for children.' 'It is even better than *When We Were Very Young*, which is saying much,' said the *Saturday Review*, and a week later May Lamberton Becker wrote in the same place: 'When the real Christopher Robin is a little old man, children will find him waiting for them. It is the child's book of the season that seems certain to stay.'

And, like the first book, it was apparently not only the child's book but the adult's book as well. It seemed Milne's books always had the double ability to open up the future for the child looking forward (filling in obscure pieces of the puzzling jigsaw that is life), and the lost past for the adult looking back. My own copy of the first edition of *Winnie-the-Pooh* was given by my father to my mother long before they had any children. 'Adults loved him first,' Elliott Graham of Dutton's told me, extravagantly. 'Every intellectual knew the books by heart. It was easily a year and a half before any children saw the books.' Earlier in the year, the *Churchman* had congratulated adults on the way they had taken the poems to their hearts. 'This book appeared in childless New York apartments, in Pullman smokers and in doctors' offices – an innocent bestseller. Mr Milne's success seems to indicate that Americans are as yet neither completely commercialised nor completely sophisticated.'

The phenomenal success of both *When We Were Very Young* and *Winnie-the-Pooh* was seen as a tribute to the mental health of thousands of Americans. One hundred and fifty thousand copies of *Winnie-the-Pooh* were sold in the United States before the end of the year. Three weeks later, Milne would say: 'In America, by the way, they seem at least twice as keen as they were on *WWWVY*' – so it seemed, though sales of the poems would keep slightly ahead of *Pooh* for many years. That was also true in Britain, where the reviews were similarly enthusiastic. 'Another book full of delight for all children under seventy,' the *Nation* said, rather strangely. (Why exclude all those over seventy?) In spite of the fact 'that it has not the advantage of demanding that it be learned by heart', it is likely 'to gain quite as many firm and unshakable admirers'. Milne would soon report that Christopher Robin himself 'knows *Winnie-the-Pooh* absolutely by heart', and there would be many like him.

Methuen had had such confidence that the first British printing was seven times the size of that of *When We Were Very Young*. In the shops on the day of publication were 32,000 copies bound in dark green cloth. Another 3,000 were bound in red, blue or green leather and there were other limited editions, specifically aimed at book collect-ors. For *Now We Are Six*, the following year, the first printing would be 50,000 and for *The House at Pooh Corner*, 75,000. Within a remarkably short time the worldwide sales of Milne's four children's books, in a multitude of languages, would be counted in millions.

6

THE END OF
A CHAPTER

Not long after *Winnie-the-Pooh* was published, the Milnes were at Cotchford for the weekend and had one of Piglet's floods on the Saturday night. They were not entirely surrounded by water (Cotchford Farm is built on the side of the valley) but the water came up to the wall at the edge of the terrace 'and from there was one large sheet of water as far as you could see in the moonlight. Unfortunately Billy was asleep, which was very unfair.' Milne resisted the temptation, writing to Ken, to quote himself: 'It wasn't much good having anything exciting like floods, if you couldn't share them with somebody.' But Daphne *was* there, gazing out at the water too; and if she was not quite as excited as the boy would have been, that was only to be expected.

He went on:

Moon tells me that Pooh is 'what I call a good sort of book',
which has encouraged me greatly. He is terribly sweet just
now – and so is Daff – and so am I – and I have just
finished with the dentist for another 9 months or so, and
am feeling rather bucked.

There was none of that terrible uncertainty about what he was going to do next. Half of the poems for *Now We Are Six* were already written and the ending of *Winnie-the-Pooh* deliberately paved the way for a sequel:

'And what did happen?' asked Christopher Robin . . .
'I don't know.'
'Could you think, and tell me and Pooh some time?'
'If you wanted it very much.'
'Pooh does,' said Christopher Robin.

Indeed, the *Evening News* Christmas edition again carried a new Pooh story, just as it had the year before. Milne had every reason to feel pleased with himself, but he could hardly believe his luck would last. He was finding the financial side of things difficult to manage. 'I feel I must save quickly, and I never know how much. It's so easy for a writer to drop out and be forgotten. I have just been helping Edwin Pugh,' he told Ken, 'who is starving and has had one article accepted in the last 18 months.' The lack of security never interfered with his generosity.

One indication of Milne's unusual reputation at this period was that he was invited to join the Athenaeum 'under the provisions of Rule II'. Most men put their names on a waiting list and waited, hoping to get there in the end. To be invited was a considerable honour and a rare one; certainly not one to be refused. Rule II required that the Members elected should be 'persons of distinguished eminence in Science, Literature, or the Arts or for Public Services' and that at the relevant meeting 'nine at least of the Committee be actually present, and the whole of those present unanimous in their Election'. Milne was rather pleased about it. He thought when he first lunched there that the denizens were more human than he expected. The *Chicago Daily Tribune*, giving the story of Milne's election, called it 'one of the most awesome and one of the most legendary places on earth'.

Writing to Swinnerton on 9 March 1928 he said: 'I feel poetical for some reason. Possibly the result of joining the Athenaeum. But I'm afraid I must chat to Sticko – I mean stick to Chatto.' Swinnerton had left the firm, after eighteen years reading for them, and was trying to persuade Milne to take his plays away. But Milne would not be persuaded. Harold Raymond, at Chatto, if not as entertaining an editor as Swinnerton, seemed keen and conscientious. Profits and sales were tiny compared with the children's books, but at least the plays were kept in print in attractive editions, which was the most important thing.

One source of income – from his manuscripts – Milne was not at all keen to exploit. When Carl Pforzheimer approached him for the manuscript of *The Ivory Door*, Daphne wrote:

My husband has found the MS of The Ivory Door *and suggests that I ask 1,000 dollars for it. He doesn't suppose that it is worth this or any other particular sum, but if it hasn't got any considerable value for anybody else, he would sooner keep it – partly from sentiment, because it is his favourite play, and partly because manuscripts sometimes get more valuable later on. Of course he will quite understand if you don't want to pay this for it – in fact he says that in your place he certainly wouldn't.*

But Pforzheimer was not to be put off. He asked for a 'special foreword' for his wife and, when that arrived, dispatched $1,000.

Milne was extremely famous, but there were still some people who had never heard of him. One night the telephone rang and Daphne said to the stranger at the other end of the line that Mr Milne was out:

STRANGER *(After apologies)* What I wanted to ask Mr Milne was, Has he any relations living in Weybridge?

DAFF: I don't think so. I've never heard of any.

S: Oh! *(With an apologetic laugh)* You see, we're having a Treasure Hunt in Weybridge, and one of the clues was something to do with A. A. Milne, so I looked him up in the Telephone Book to see his Weybridge address, and found that he lived in Chelsea, so I wondered if any of his family—

D: But surely it referred to one of his books?

S: His what?

D: Books!

S: I'm sorry—

D: Books!

S: *(bewildered)* Oh!

D: You knew he was the well-known author—

S: The what?

D: AUTHOR!

S: Oh! . . . Oh, well, you see, I'm afraid that's not much in my line, all that sort of thing. Thanks so much. Sorry to have troubled you for nothing.

Good-bye. *(Exit to resume hunt – but I doubt if he was successful.)*

The Milne phone number was obviously not ex-directory and there would sometimes be calls from strangers with hard-luck stories. There would also be begging letters, among the piles of praise and requests for articles, appearances, autographs. It was now that Milne began to develop the habit Christopher Milne described of doing nothing about some things – which, as Owl said wisely, was sometimes the best thing. But Milne had plenty of charitable impulses: he gave generously both to the Royal Literary Fund for indigent writers and the Society of Authors Pension Fund. He would often write something for good causes. In a sense, it was guilt money. He would say how easy it was to give money, how difficult to do anything for those worse off than ourselves. At least writing fundraising letters was more worthwhile than just writing cheques. He raised funds for the Children's Country Holiday Fund, writing regular annual letters about the scheme in *The Times*. In one he said, 'Ladies may regret their last hat, and a man the new brassie which has not added twenty yards to his drive. The only money which we are never sorry to have spent is the money which we have given away.'

Milne supported Toc H. In one appeal he wrote for

Tubby Clayton, he expressed again his feeling that no one should congratulate themselves as having earned their good fortune, no one can claim to be a self-made man. 'Idiots we are, if we can look at ourselves, however high our achievements, however great our success, with anything but humility and thankfulness. Our achievements, our possessions, are not of our own making; they were given to us. There is only one honest answer to that hackneyed question of the interviewer: "To what do you attribute your success?" And the answer is "Luck!"' He appealed to people to say thank you for their good fortune by helping others who had been less lucky.

On another occasion, he wrote an extremely successful appeal letter on behalf of a hospital, signing thousands of letters and writing hundreds of thank-yous. It began like this:

I expect you know the story of the man who took his friend to the bar, and said, with a large and generous air, 'Now then, what would you like?' – to which the friend replied that he thought he would like a pint of champagne. 'Oh!' said his host, 'Well, try thinking of something nearer threepence.'

What the Hampstead General Hospital would like is £10,000, and it would be a simplification of

*its finances if you were charming enough to send
them a cheque for that amount in the enclosed
envelope; but if you would prefer to think of
something nearer threepence I shall understand.
Not near enough to give you the bother of buying
stamps or postal orders; something in guineas, I
suggest, which will give you no more trouble than
the opening of your cheque-book. But just as you
like, so long as you help us.*

Milne drew the line at appearing at the Savoy luncheon or the Mayfair Hotel dinner in connection with the appeal. He rarely appeared in public. 'I may be unique in not wanting to say anything aloud at any time,' he once said, and on another occasion: 'I dislike public appearances, always avoid them, and am, in fact, not very good at them.' '"Some can and some can't, that's how it is", as Christopher Robin's friend, Pooh, used to say,' Milne quoted, at a time when he was still quoting Pooh. (There would be times when the very name would make him shudder.)

With the extraordinary success of the children's books, Milne altered his life in no way at all. He had completed the purchase of Cotchford Farm almost at the very moment that *When We Were Very Young* was published. He had no wish for any larger or grander home either in London or the country. Both houses were comfortably equipped and furnished and staffed. He ran a good enough car (later there would be another, which stayed permanently at Cotchford) and employed a chauffeur. Milne said he had inherited from his father a love not of money but of not having to worry about it, of being extravagant in a thoroughly sensible way. 'We set our standards within our income and then enjoyed them carelessly . . . I shouldn't be happy if I couldn't be reckless about golf-balls, taxis, the best seats at cricket grounds and theatres, shirts and pullovers, tips, subscriptions, books and wine-lists.' He liked buying expensive lingerie for Daphne at Christmas, going to Harvey Nichols, consulting the assistants and choosing with enormous care – 'soft, pretty crêpe-de-chiney, lacey things. What fun!' He enjoyed these minor extravagances. (Daphne would enjoy more major extravagances of her own.) He made sure he was always salting enough away not only for the future of his own family, but for Ken's as well.

Milne never gambled, but he would put up money for something he thought worth doing. For instance, in the summer of 1928 his friend P. G. Wodehouse was looking for an extra backer for Ian Hay's dramatisation of his novel *A Damsel in Distress*. Wodehouse wrote: 'The management, Ian and I are each putting up £500. We needed another £500 to make up the necessary £2,000 and A. A. Milne gallantly stepped forward and said he would like to come in. I don't think we shall lose our money as Ian has done an awfully good job.' It indeed proved a safe investment.

Milne had taken on the responsibility for Ken's family with a real joy that he was able to do it. 'CVSD' (*ça va sans dire*) he would say to Ken, over and over again, when some question of education or medical expenses came up. They were such a rewarding family. 'I love you all,' he ended one letter to Ken and obviously meant it. At the end of another letter he wrote, 'You must be very proud of your family. So am I – I mean of yours, but also of mine. He is a darling. Much too good for me. So is Daff.' (Viola Tree had just described him in the *Woman's Pictorial* as 'a natural bachelor'. 'For a natural bachelor I have done well,' he wrote. Certainly, a great deal better than Kenneth Grahame, that other 'natural bachelor'.)

It was fortunate for both families that he had done so well financially. But he never let his riches go to his head. He remained sensible about money. Christopher Milne would say, 'There was something not quite nice about being rich.' A. A. Milne could hardly believe that he was or that, if he really was, that he would remain so. He always had the feeling at the back of his mind that in some mysterious way it would suddenly stop, that no one would buy his books or produce his plays and he would have to live on his savings. One of Ken's children remembered that he always read bills carefully before paying them and was often appalled by high prices (a relic surely of the time when he first came to London). He would be amazed at the cost of Christopher's school clothes or of a particular restaurant ('Gosh, this costs more than the Mirabelle!') and his niece once caught him out in an extraordinary small economy, 're-using last year's diary, altering the days'. Perhaps it was really just that he had kept forgetting to buy a new one until the point when there were none left in the shops. He sometimes failed to realise just how short of money Ken's daughters were when they were first working in London. He would ask them to dinner at Mallord Street before the theatre, forgetting how the cost of the taxi, which they would need to take because of their theatre-going clothes and the time factor, meant that they would have to cut down on their lunches for a week.

J. V. Milne took a particular pleasure in his son's new kind of success. It was as if he had been waiting all the time for the children's books. He relished every sales figure, every sign of their widespread fame (Pooh prints being given away with *Home Chat*, 'Vespers' being sung on the wireless). Alan wrote to Ken: 'Father seems so terribly happy and excited that he makes me feel ashamed of not having made him happy before.'

Christopher Robin had other things on his mind besides Pooh, now that he was six and a half. His world was expanding. Someone had given him a map of Africa, which hung on the wall of his bedroom and fed his imagination. One day he would travel far further than A. A. Milne ever had. Books fed his mind too. 'Moon is devoted to the *Children's Encyclopaedia*, which I gave him at Christmas, and brings a volume down to breakfast whenever he comes. Flags, beetles and the inside of engines seem to be his favourite reading.' Years before, Milne had surprised a nursery of Ken's children similarly absorbed. He had gone up expecting to have to impersonate a bear but had found there was no demand for bears. 'Each child lay on its front, engrossed in a volume of the *Children's Encyclopaedia*. Nobody looked up as I came in. Greatly relieved, I also took a volume of the great work and lay down on my front.' He considered many of the answers were aimed more at him than at the children.

Take a question like 'Why does a stone sink?' No

child wants to know why a stone sinks; it knows the answer already – 'What else could it do?' Even Sir Isaac Newton was grown up before he asked why an apple fell, and there had been men in the world fifty thousand years before that, none of whom bothered his head about gravity.

Christopher was particularly concerned about his wildlife, and not just beetles. He went off to stay with the Darlingtons on one occasion, taking the volume containing CATERPILLARS with him, much to his father's dismay when he wanted to check on a curious caterpillar he had found in Christopher's absence. Was it a Death's Head Hawk Moth? It was certainly bigger than a Poplar Hawk. He wrote to Ken that it 'Looked exactly like a small snake in marking and colouring . . . and the *Enc. Britt.* isn't very forthcoming on the subject.'

Now We Are Six was slowly taking shape. Milne wrote to Shepard after a day at Methuen, 'Muller and I got to work on the book today, and I saw the new drawings. At present we have pasted up 14, taking 42 pages.' Milne told Shepard how much space he was reckoning 'for some of the poems which you have still to do'. He planned, for instance, that 'Forgiven', the one about Alexander Beetle, should take up three pages, giving Shepard the chance to draw the disappearing beetle over and over again as he runs away and disappears off the page. But it didn't work out quite right. It should have been a right-hand page. As it is, poor Alexander Beetle looks as if he has been cut in two.

Milne was slightly worried about the length of the new book. In the end, it turned out to be a couple of pages longer than *When We Were Very Young*, though there were nine poems fewer. Shepard was already working on the second collection of Pooh stories. Milne had bought another new character and looked forward to seeing him for the first time: 'I'm longing to see the "Tigger" illustrations,' he wrote. Shepard had introduced the toys into the illustrations for *Now We Are Six* far more than Milne had into the poems themselves. Pooh goes nearly everywhere that Christopher Robin goes, of course, as Milne suggests in 'Us Two':

> *Wherever I am, there's always Pooh,*
> *There's always Pooh and Me.*
> *Whatever I do, he wants to do,*
> *'Where are you going today?' says Pooh:*
> *'Well, that's very odd 'cos I was too.*
> *'Let's go together,' says Pooh, says he.*
> *'Let's go together,' says Pooh.*

Christopher Robin, as seen by E. H. Shepard in the last chapter of *The House at Pooh Corner* and as photographed by his father in 1924, apparently 'examining a butterfly'.

A. A. Milne in uniform before leaving for the Somme in July 1916. He wrote afterwards about 'a nightmare of mental and moral degradation'.

Father and son: A. A. and C. R. Milne. The child was always known as Billy.

Christopher Robin
and Pooh.

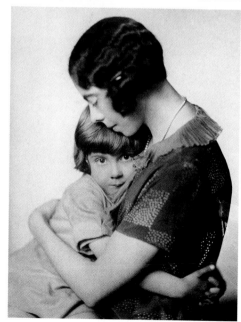

Christopher Robin with
his mother, Daphne.

Christopher Robin with his nanny, Olive Rand, known to him as 'Nou'. She holds Pooh; a larger Piglet is by the fence.

At London Zoo with Winnie the Canadian bear, who gave Pooh his name, March 1927.

Poohsticks Bridge,
as seen by E. H.
Shepard in 1926
and more recently.

Of course as soon as Kanga unbuttoned her pocket, she saw what had happened. Just for a moment she thought she was frightened, and then she knew she wasn't; for she felt quite sure that Christopher Robin would never let any harm happen to Roo. So she said to herself, "If they are having a joke with me, I will have a joke with them."

"Now then, Roo, dear," she said, as she took Piglet out of her pocket. "Bed-time?"

"Aha!" said Piglet, as well as he could after his Terrifying Journey. But it wasn't a very good "Aha!" and Kanga didn't seem to understand what it meant.

"Bath first," said Kanga in a cheerful voice.

"Aha!" said Piglet again, looking round anxiously for the others. But the others weren't there. Rabbit was playing with Baby Roo in his own house, and feeling more fond of him every minute, and Pooh, who had decided to be Kanga, was still at the sandy place on the top of the Forest, practising jumps.

"I am not at all sure," said Kanga in a thoughtful voice, "that it wouldn't be a good idea to have a cold bath this evening. Would you like that, Roo, dear?"

Piglet, who had never been really fond of baths, shuddered a long indignant shudder, and said in as brave a voice as he could: "Kanga, I see that the time has come to speak plainly."

"Funny little Roo," said Kanga, as she got the bath-water ready.

68

A page of the manuscript of *Winnie-the-Pooh*,
given by Milne to his old college, Trinity, Cambridge.

Christopher Robin and Pooh by Marcus Adams, March 1928.

The toys in their home in the Children's Room of the New York Public Library, looking their age. They have recently been tenderly repaired.

The front of Cotchford Farm, Hartfield, thirty-five miles
from London, bought by Milne in 1925.

The back lawn at Cotchford, with Daphne, Christopher Robin,
Pooh and Alan Milne looking distinctly uneasy.

He goes along, just as he always did, with Anne and Christopher on their morning walk. But Eeyore and Piglet and Kanga and Roo are there from time to time too. They wait on the platform in 'The Engineer'. They had become such public figures they could hardly be left out entirely. Methuen's advance publicity would say the new book was 'better' than *When We Were Very Young*. 'This is doubtful,' Milne said – but he thought it 'pretty much as good as'. Certainly, it contained a number of poems – 'King John's Christmas', 'Sneezles', 'The Old Sailor' and 'In the Dark', for instance – as memorable as anything in the earlier book.

With four of the *House at Pooh Corner* stories under his belt, Milne was spending August at Cotchford working on a play – 'a Detective Play which is fun to do'. Plays were always fun to do. The awful part came afterwards. Negotiations for *The Ivory Door* were still going on. That was the 'Shakespearean' one – the costume play with masses of characters. There was the possibility it might be done that autumn in both New York and London. In the event it opened in New York in October – but it was not until April 1929, after the detective play, that it came on in London. 'I have given up bothering about it,' Milne told Ken, but it was still very close to his heart. A headline in a Canadian paper the year before (of a review of his Chatto volume *Four Plays*) read:

A. A. MILNE'S STAR IS NOW IN ASCENDANT AS PLAYWRIGHT

It was hardly a snappy headline and he knew, in any case, it was not true. Already too many people were thinking of him primarily as a children's writer. A review of the same book in *Granta* began:

> I think Mr Milne, at some time in his career, must have whispered to himself, ever so gently, 'One day, I shall write a great play'; and I'm also certain that after completing this volume, he whispered, even more gently, 'I shall never write a great play.'

The volume included *Success*, one of the plays for which Milne had had such particularly high hopes. The *Granta* reviewer liked it too. 'In parts there is a vigour and a strength, which in spite of all the doubts, leave a hope; and I have hoped for and enjoyed Mr Milne for so long that I can't give up the habit. Perhaps, after all, he hasn't whispered that second sentence.' I think, in fact, that he had. There is no way, really, that a 'detective play' can be a 'great play'. He would write half a dozen more plays. He would never write a great play.

The Fourth Wall, which would be produced in New York as *The Perfect Alibi*, was certainly an ingenious play – 'an exceedingly interesting one from a technical point of view. In the first act it shows us a murder. We see the crime committed and who has done it. In the second and third acts we watch the other characters trying to unravel the mystery. Such a scheme is, of course, the very opposite of what generally happens in "detective plays" . . . Courage and originality of treatment are things to be thankful for, and for their sakes I rank *The Fourth Wall* as far above any other "detective play" I have seen,' one reviewer would say. The bus-boards would read 'the best murder in London' in a season when nearly every first act contained a corpse.

But in the summer of 1927 Milne was really not worrying about anything as he sat in a deck chair on the lawn at Cotchford, writing to Ken:

We are terribly happy here. I could go on and on doing nothing but watch Daff weed, and she could go on and on weeding. Really the garden is lovely now, and I wish you and Maud could see it. We have just been ordering our next year's improvements. I shall leave something beautiful behind anyway. Moon had a tent, two bantams and a rope-ladder among his birthday presents. The lady bantam laid her first egg yesterday, and he has just eaten it. He knows the name of every flower in the garden; and when the expert horticulturist points to a small green, as yet unflowering, bush, and says 'What's that? I don't think I know that?' Moon pipes up, 'Zauschneria – or Californian fuchsia'. And he not only knows but can spell Eschscholtzia, which nobody else can do.

Now We Are Six was published on 13 October in both Britain and America. Christopher Robin's copy was inscribed:

> *For my Moon*
> *From his Blue*
> *Now I am 45*

Milne wrote to tell Ken in November: 'The reviews have been poor in England but much better in America. If I were a critic I should loathe A. A. Milne. How could one help wanting to say that he was falling off, or taking success too easily or whatnot? However this is the end of the verses; and then, after one more *Pooh* book, I must think of something else. In fact, it's time I tried a novel.' The reviews were mixed, with plenty of critics in both countries enjoying the new book. In Britain, the *Spectator* said: 'The severest criticism that can possibly be made . . . is that it does not quite reach the extraordinarily high standard he has set himself.' In America, the *New York Times* said that it might not be 'as fresh as *When We Were Very Young* but it comes close'.

In fact, it did not matter very much what the reviews said. On both sides of the Atlantic, the new book sold immediately and enormously on the strength of the earlier book of poems. At Christmas, J. V. Milne was able to write to his friend, Miss Pinnington: 'The success of Alan's books is remarkable.' He set out these British sales figures:

Now We Are Six	94,000
Winnie-the-Pooh	80,000
When We Were Very Young	169,000

So the new book, not much more than two months after publication, had already overtaken the bestselling *Winnie-the-Pooh*, published a year earlier.

At Christmas, Milne looked back on the year. Things were good. '*The Ivory Door* goes on well in New York, playing to bigger houses each week, and should be in for a good run. But it had to fight its way against the seas of

Sex and Crime which pour down Broadway at the moment, and nearly got swamped. Talking of Crime, the Haymarket has just taken my detective play.' It would open on 29 February 1928 – the day after a revival of *Mr Pim Passes By* at the St Martin's, with Marie Tempest in Irene Vanbrugh's old part. 'Having had no play in London for three years', Milne rather wished *The Ivory Door* was coming on first, but *The Fourth Wall* would be far more successful than *The Ivory Door*.

Life was a little overshadowed in December 1927 because 'our beloved Moon has chicken-pox' – not too badly, but 'he was to have sung various solos and duets at his school breaking-up and now he won't. We were looking forward to it more eagerly than to any first night of mine. He sings jolly well.'

He did indeed, well enough only a little later to make a recording of four of the poems Fraser-Simson had set to music.

When the idea first came up, the following argument took place, or so Milne would lead Ken to believe:

ME: (when it was first suggested) Bah!
DAFF: It will be a Wonderful Thing to Have!
ME: Who is Moon? . . . I'm the only important person in this house. Christopher Robin doesn't exist. He is a

pigment-figment of the imagination. Why should a small unimportant boy—

DAFF: It would be a Wonderful Thing to Have – Afterwards.

ME: After what?

DAFF: I mean—

ME: Now if they'd asked Me—

DAFF: I thought you said they did?

ME: Oh! I didn't know I'd told you that.

DAFF: I wish you would! It would be a Wonderful Thing to Have – Afterwards.

ME: After what?

DAFF: I mean—

ME: I think the Whole thing is Perfectly Disgusting; I'll have Nothing to do with it. You can do what you like about it. I wash my hands of it. (Exit to bathroom.) So Daff went to the Gramophone Co., they all fell on her neck—

and the record was the result. Whether the whole idea was Daphne's own, as this suggests, we don't know for certain.

One of Christopher's cousins remembered the record well and thought it 'the unacceptable face of Poohdom'. That was not so much 'the sound of the record as the idea'. As for the record itself, 'it was the voice of a small boy who was obviously musical – dead in tune and sweet of tone – and who was obviously giving the performance all he'd got. (Perhaps this added to my feeling that the poor child was being exploited.) There were four songs – "Vespers", "Buckingham Palace", "Fishing" and the one about the train brake that didn't work.'

There were preliminary rehearsals in the first-floor drawing-room at Mallord Street (the room with the golden walls), a final practice in the Fraser-Simsons' house round the corner (with some coaching from Cicely Fraser-Simson, to whom *The Hums of Pooh* would be dedicated in 1929) – and then to the HMV studio. In fact, there must have been two records, for the one that Christopher remembered included 'The Friend'. He had to put on a Poohish voice when he sang: 'Well, *I* say sixpence, but I don't suppose I'm right.' Rather a difficult thing to do.

It was 'Vespers', however, that returned to haunt him years later when boys in the next study at Stowe would play it over and over again, remorselessly. It was 'intensely painful' for the singer. 'Eventually the joke, if not the record, wore out, they handed it to me' (the record not the joke) 'and I took it and broke it into a hundred fragments and scattered them over a distant field.' Years later, his cousin Angela allowed her children to hang the record on a tree, a string through the hole in the middle, and to throw things at it. One wonders how many copies remain in attics along with Ernest Lush singing 'O for the Wings of a Dove' and Harry Lauder's 'I Love a Lassie'.

Christopher had another important part in the spring of 1928. Milne wrote to Ken:

> *Daff is terribly busy, and so am I up to a point, in arranging this Pooh party. Beginning with no more than a kindly interest in the proceedings, and a gracious permission to certain performers to sing certain songs, we have got more and more dragged into it, until now we provide the whole programme, company, organisation and everything else. Moon makes three appearances – besides acting as host and shaking hands with the 350 odd guests! (We have told him to ooze away at about the 50th.) He sings* The Friend *with Pooh by his side – delightfully and really funnily. He recites with another small boy (W. G. Stevens' son)* Us Two, *and he plays in Eeyore's Birthday the part which is Owl's in the book, but has been made Christopher Robin's in the play. He loves it, is quite unshy, and speaks beautifully. Piglet is played by a darling little fat girl, Veronica, aged 4, with a very deep voice*

which comes out loudly and suddenly on all the
unimportant words – 'Many happy returns OF the
day' – 'Perhaps EEYORE doesn't like BALLOONS
so very VERY much' – it's frightfully funny, and
she looks superb. Eeyore is Anne Hastings Turner
– terribly bad, but from sheer vanity may pull it off
on the afternoon – and Pooh is the Stevens boy, also
quite unshy and intelligent, but unfortunately with
rather a niminy-piminy voice, quite unlike Pooh's
gruff voice as inspired by Moon. Anne Darlington,
alas, wasn't allowed to appear, as she gets too excited
and upsets herself. Dress rehearsal this afternoon.
We burst two balloons at every rehearsal, which
seems rather a pity.

And in July 1929 there would be a pageant in Ashdown
Forest twice a day for four days. The Mackails would go
down with the Milnes ('the sun nearly roasted us to
death,' Mackail foolishly complained) to see Christopher
Robin (afternoons only) playing himself and the children of Park House School playing 'Winnie-the-Pooh
and the other toys'. There would be a procession as the
finale of the pageant – which included practically every
historical character you could think of: Earl Godwin,
Queen Elizabeth, Nell Gwynn, Cromwell, Lady Hamilton,

Wellington ... And then, in among them, there was Christopher Robin and the children representing 'Ashdown Forest today where a boy and his bear will always be playing'. Christopher enjoyed it: 'Exciting without being frightening. For there was nothing to be nervous about, nothing to go wrong. It was not like acting in a play or making a gramophone record when your voice might go funny.' There was nothing to go wrong. But for Milne himself, by July 1929, everything had gone wrong.

We have leapt ahead, following the boy in his starring roles, enjoying for the last time his part as Christopher Robin. Now we must go back and look further at the children's books – *Now We Are Six* and *The House at Pooh Corner* – which were keeping them all so firmly in the public eye, on both sides of the Atlantic.

In America, 90,000 copies of *Now We Are Six* had already been ordered on publication day in October 1927. The *Retail Bookseller* said it was 'another unquestionable bullseye'. It was top of the general bestseller list during its first month on sale. 'For the third time A. A. Milne has demonstrated that a book for children can outsell all other books in the country.'

One strong voice stood out against the general murmur

of pleasure. Dorothy Parker, disguised as 'Constant Reader', mounted her first attack. In the *New Yorker* on 12 November 1927 she had great fun with two new children's books – *Now We Are Six* and Christopher Morley's *I Know a Secret*, which the publishers had claimed to be fit to stand in the company of *Alice*, *Peter Pan* and *When We Were Very Young*. Mrs Parker said she found it difficult not to confuse Christopher Morley with Christopher Robin. Indeed, she found that:

> during those fretful hours when I am tossing and turning at my typewriter, during the mellow evenings, during the dim, drowsy watches of the night, my mind goes crooning:
>
> > Christopher Morley goes hippety, hoppety
> > Hippety, hippety, hop.
> > Whenever I ask him politely to stop it, he
> > Says he can't possibly stop . . .
>
> The thing is too much for me. I am about to give it all up. I cannot get those two quaint kiddies straightened out.

But Mrs Parker doesn't give up. She goes on and on and on, just like the tail of Christopher Robin's dormouse.

She says if anyone had addressed her, as Morley does, as 'dear my urchin', when she was a little one, she would have doubled her dimpled fist 'and socked him one right on the button', and we can well believe it. Morley's book 'set new standards of whimsy, plumbed new depths of quaintness'. Unlike *Now We Are Six*, it has sunk without trace and was hardly worth Mrs Parker wasting her typewriter ribbon. When she finally leaves Morley and gets to Milne, it goes like this:

While we are on the subject of whimsies, how about taking up Mr A. A. Milne? There is a strong feeling, I know, that to speak against Mr Milne puts one immediately in the ranks of those who set fire to orphanages, strike crippled newsboys, and lure little curly-heads off into corners to explain to them that Santa Claus is only Daddy making a fool of himself. But I too have a very strong feeling about the Whimsicality of Milne. I'm feeling it right this minute. It's in my stomach.

Time was when A. A. Milne was my only hero. Weekly I pounced on *Punch* for the bits signed 'A. A. M.' I kept 'Once a Week' and 'Half Hours' [she means 'Happy Days' presumably] practically under my pillow. I read 'The Red House Mystery' threadbare. I thought 'The Truth about Blayds' a fine and merciless and honest play. But when Mr Milne went quaint, all was over. Now he leads his life and I lead mine.

'Now We Are Six', the successor to 'When We Were Very Young', is Mr Milne gone completely Winnie-the-Pooh. Not since Fay Bainter played 'East is West' have I seen such sedulous cuteness. I give you, for example, the postscript to the preface: 'Pooh wants us to say that he thought it was a different book; and he hopes you won't mind, but he walked through it one day, looking for his friend Piglet, and sat down on some of the pages by mistake.' That one sentence may well make Christopher Morley stamp on his pen in despair. A. A. Milne still remains the Master.

Of Milne's recent verse, I speak in a minority amounting to solitude. I think it is affected, commonplace, bad. I did so, too, say bad. And now I must stop, to get ready for being ridden out of town on a rail.

CONSTANT READER

Anne Darlington could be numbered among those unspeakable characters who reveal the awful fact that Father Christmas does not exist; Christopher Milne could still point out the exact place where one morning on the way to the kindergarten in Tite Street with their nannies, Anne made her revelation. *Now We Are Six* is dedicated to Anne:

TO

ANNE DARLINGTON

NOW SHE IS SEVEN

AND

BECAUSE SHE IS

SO

SPESHAL

That spelling of 'special' has made other gorges rise besides Mrs Parker's. Somehow it seems all right when Christopher Robin can't spell and leaves his famous note:

GON OUT

BACKSON

BISY

BACKSON

When Milne himself pretends he can't spell, there is a good deal of revulsion from even his most dedicated admirers. But his inscription in Anne Darlington's own copy of the book is beautifully turned and shows clearly his special devotion to the child:

> *This book of songs*
> *Dear Anne, belongs to you.*
> *It carries much*
> *Of love and such from Blue.*
> *And for the rest*
> *It says as best it can*
> *'Be never far*
> *From Moon, my darling Anne.'*

Her father, W. A. Darlington, would remember the children playing on the nursery floor in Mallord Street with Daphne who 'helped to bring the toy animals to life and give them their character'. He said that Alan Milne 'never joined in their games but watched them with delight'. Christopher's nanny, as we saw, remembered Milne himself entering into the games; he 'spoke to the toys as if they were real people'. Both could be right. Other days, other moods. Christopher would remember that he and his mother and the toys played together, 'and gradually more life, more character flowed into them, until they reached a point at which my father could take over. Then, as the first stories were written, the cycle was repeated. The Pooh in my arms, the Pooh sitting opposite me at the breakfast table was a Pooh who had climbed trees in search of honey, who had got stuck in a rabbit hole . . .'

Certainly, from Milne's letters one would imagine that all the ideas for the stories came entirely from Milne's head (together with Owl and Rabbit) and that it was only the toy animals themselves which came from the nursery – their characters and voices certainly owing a good deal to Christopher himself and Daphne. Daphne was undoubtedly obsessed by the pretence that Pooh and the others were alive. There is a rather rebarbative glimpse of her in a gushing article by the American May Lamberton Becker, who had first met the Milnes a few years earlier and had sent Christopher a marvellous Indian headdress as a present. Daphne's ecstatic thanks perhaps gives a flavour of her talk: 'Christopher Robin was simply too enchanted . . . It was really lovely of you to remember him and he does thank you ever so much . . . I do wish you could see him going out in it, he does look such a duck.' Gushing seemed to be the flavour of the time . . . In 1928 Miss Becker came more as a friend than a reporter. When she arrived, Christopher was attacking his father with boxing gloves:

A long nursery with walls the colour of sunshine; an eminent author crouched in the window-seat, clutching to his breast a fat yellow sofa-cushion; facing him at a convenient distance for attack, a little boy in boxing-gloves, his golden hair tossed back from the brightest and brownest eyes in London, his feet tapping back and forth in the proper professional preparations.

The real Christopher Robin still looks like Mr Shepard's pictures; that is, in moments of comparative repose, and when completing a particularly good tea at the round table in the yellow nursery. But only a cinema, an earnest one up to its business, could deal with Christopher Robin's boxing. It is the real thing and no mistake. Besides his school, he now goes to a famous gymnasium – oh yes, he's still a little boy, but when you say he is, you should stress the second word instead of the first.

As I watched the pillow take punishment, a small, gruff voice – the voice Pooh uses when Mrs Milne is in the room – cried 'Here! hold me up! I mustn't miss this!' and a brown bear came tumbling over my shoulder down into my lap. I had him right-side up directly; I kept my cheek on his good comfortable head for the rest of the bout. I was thinking of the

American children whose eyes would shine when I told them, 'It was just this way that I held Pooh in my arms so he could watch Christopher Robin boxing.'

Pooh has been told that there will be no more books about him after this one that is just coming, *The House at Pooh Corner*. I do not know if he has quite taken it in; ideas come rather slowly to Pooh, and he makes no special effort to assimilate unpleasant ideas. What! retire from literature just when one has performed the unprecedented feat of changing the name of a household institution on the other side of the earth? for this is what happened when almost over night all the Teddy-bears of America became Pooh-bears in the vocabulary of childhood.

It seems there are to be positively no more Christopher Robin books. Mr Milne says so, and he ought to know. 'No, more Christopher Robin books!' said Mrs Milne. 'Look, Pooh's crying!' And indeed the brown bear in her arms had his paws over his face. But between them his candid eyes looked out confidently. Pooh knows that his place in literature is safe.

Claude Luke, another visitor that year, gave readers in *John o'London's* a further view of the happy family in the sunny house in Chelsea which somehow, mysteriously, seemed full of the 'breath of morning, morning in a very young world'. After some lamenting over 'the tragic ephemerality of such splendid childhood', Luke yet managed to convey a very realistic small boy and his nursery – the animals ('not the original Piglet which, alas, had been chewed by a dog' and replaced by one of more suitable size), the books, including *Dr Dolittle*, the walls hung with Shepard drawings, a coloured *Spy* sketch of his father, that pictorial map of Africa, that Indian headdress. When Luke asked him the obvious question about whether he liked his father's books, instead of doubling up his dimpled fist as the young Dorothy Parker would have done, Christopher Robin just 'gazed at me for a moment, amazed at the immense foolishness of humans and then turned to his nurse with the expressive remark, "Do I, Nanny?" as though to say, "Throw out this absurd man!"'

When Nanny had gone downstairs to see about lunch, Christopher favoured Mr Luke with a glimpse of a row of bottles in a secret corner:

'They're my poisons!' he whispered, in a voice that would have thrilled Edgar Wallace. I read the labels inscribed in a childish scrawl. One was 'Salerd dressing for letters'; another 'Cind of frute salerd – it is good to drink'; and a third 'Loshun for the mouth'. He opened one for me to smell.

'I can't face that one,' he admitted, wryly, and confessed that it was composed of ipecacuanha wine, flour paste, and ink! We agreed it had a deadly odour.

It was all getting a bit much. The time had obviously come to call a halt, to bring the whole business to an end. Milne would try, but as May Lambert Becker had said, 'Pooh's place in literature was safe', and that meant that Christopher Robin would never go away either. Somehow the real boy, whose name had been taken, would have to continue to live with him, would have, eventually, to come to terms with him.

The House at Pooh Corner was published in both New York and London in October 1928. On the British jacket the totals of the sales were now:

When We Were Very Young	179th thousand
Winnie-the-Pooh	96th thousand
Now We Are Six	109th thousand

In America they were correspondingly larger. The reviews in both countries were almost unanimously enthusiastic. Everyone had been told it was the last book and again and again reviewers lamented the fact. *Punch* said: 'The last book is as good as the first. It is too bad that Christopher Robin has to grow up.' The *Saturday Review*: 'The stories have lost none of their charm. It is a shame to see them end.' Even the *Times Literary Supplement*, although it congratulated Milne on deciding to avoid 'the temptation to repeat his successful formula mechanically', said: 'It is sad to see the stories end.' Only Dorothy Parker, the Constant Reader, returning to her attack of the previous year, poured scorn on Pooh's hum, the one about 'The more it snows, tiddely-pom'. It was an easy target:

It 'seemed to him a Good Hum, such as is Hummed Hopefully to Others.' In fact, so Good a Hum did it seem that he and Piglet started right out through the snow to Hum It Hopefully to Eeyore. Oh, darn – there I've gone and given away the plot. Oh, I could bite my tongue out.

As they are trotting along against the flakes, Piglet begins to weaken a bit.

'"Pooh," he said at last and a little timidly, because he didn't want Pooh to think he was Giving In, "I was just wondering. How would it be if we went home now and practised your song, and then sang it to Eeyore tomorrow – or – the next day, when we happen to see him."

"'That's a very good idea, Piglet," said Pooh. "We'll practise it now as we go along. But it's no good going home to practise it, because it's a special Outdoor Song which Has To Be Sung In The Snow."

"'Are you sure?" asked Piglet anxiously.

"'Well, you'll see, Piglet, when you listen. Because this is how it begins. The more it snows, tiddely-pom–"

"'Tiddely what?" said Piglet.' (He took, as you might say, the very words out of your correspondent's mouth.)

"'Pom," said Pooh. "I put that in to make it more hummy."'

And it is that word 'hummy', my darlings, that marks the first place in *The House at Pooh Corner* at which Tonstant Weader fwowed up.

Milne hated it, of course. He had resisted the temptation to reply the year before and now he would wait more than ten years. In his autobiography he wrote:

The books were written for children. When, for instance, Dorothy Parker, as 'Constant Reader' in *The New Yorker*, delights the sophisticated by announcing that at page 5 of *The House of Pooh Corner* 'Tonstant Weader fwowed up' (sic, if I may), she leaves the book, oddly enough, much where it was. However greatly indebted to Mrs Parker, no Alderney, at the approach of the milkmaid, thinks 'I hope this lot will turn out to be gin', no writer of children's books says gaily to his publisher, 'Don't bother about the children, Mrs Parker will love it.'

Milne had made the decision to stop long before Mrs Parker. She simply added to his satisfaction in his own decision, so clearly included in the book itself. At the end of *The House at Pooh Corner*, shades of the prison house are beginning to close around Christopher Robin; it is all coming to an end. School and growing up are claiming the boy as they claim every child. Things would never be the same again.

That Christmas, Christopher had his first pair of football boots and wore them in the house, 'so as to get used to them'. In January 1929, just three months after the book was published, he started at prep school, at Gibbs' in Sloane Square, in a bright red blazer, with a bright red cap on his newly trimmed hair. Nanny took him in the number 11 bus along the King's Road. Milne wrote to Ken:

> *Moon is in the thick of school life. Daff thinks he's aged ten years. I don't think it's quite as bad as this,*

*and anyway, if he's 12 one moment, he's 2 the next.
Also instead of saying 'No, Blosh' (corruption of
'Blue') when I tell him to do anything, he now says
'Yes, sir' and does it. But somehow I fancy that the
novelty of this will wear off. He is very happy, and
began Latin and French on the same day, and is
now grappling (a little prematurely, I think) with
the domestic life of the four Georges.*

It was time to leave the Forest. As Christopher Robin said to Pooh:

'I'm not going to do Nothing any more.'
'Never again?'
'Well, not so much. They don't let you.'

This is not sentimental. It is an occasion for real feeling and, if we cannot accept it, it is our fault, not Milne's. It is only in the memory that 'a little boy and his Bear will always be playing', as the final often-quoted words of the last children's book have it.

To stop while the going was good, that was the point; and, if possible, to protect his son from any further glare of publicity. In 1929 Milne wrote at length, and cogently, about the reasons behind his decision. He had been amazed at the way readers, back in 1924, had singled out the child:

> You can imagine my amazement and disgust, then, when I discovered that in a night, so to speak, I had been pushed into a back place, and that the hero of *When We Were Very Young* was not, as I had modestly expected, the author, but a curiously named child of whom, at this time, I had scarcely heard. It was this Christopher Robin who kept mice, walked on the lines and not in the squares, and wondered what to do on a spring morning; it was this Christopher Robin, not I, whom Americans were clamouring to see; and in fact (to make due acknowledgement at last), it was this Christopher Robin, not I, not the publishers, who was selling the book in such large and ridiculous quantities.
>
> Now who was this Christopher Robin – the hero now, since it was so accepted, of *When We Were Very Young*, soon to be the hero of *Winnie-the-Pooh* and two other books? To me he was, and remained, the child of my imagination. When I thought of him, I thought of him in the Forest, living in his tree as no child really lives; not in the nursery, where a differently named child (so far as we in this house are concerned) was

playing with his animals. For this reason I have not felt self-conscious when writing about him, nor apologetic at the thought of exposing my own family to the public gaze. The 'animals', Pooh and Piglet, Eeyore, Kanga, and the rest, are in a different case. I have not 'created' them. He and his mother gave them life, and I have just 'put them into a book'. You can see them now in the nursery, as Ernest Shepard saw them before he drew them. Between us, it may be, we have given them shape, but you have only to look at them to see, as I saw at once, that Pooh is a Bear of Very Little Brain, Tigger Bouncy, Eeyore Melancholy and so on. I have exploited them for my own profit, as I feel I have not exploited the legal Christopher Robin. All I have got from Christopher Robin is a name which he never uses, an introduction to his friends ... and a gleam which I have tried to follow.

However, the distinction, if clear to me, is not so clear to others; and to them, anyhow, perhaps to me also, the dividing line between the imaginary and the legal Christopher Robin becomes fainter with each book. This, then, brings me (at last) to one of the reasons why these verses and stories have come to an end. I feel that the legal Christopher Robin has already had more publicity than I want for him. Moreover, since he is growing up, he will soon feel that he has had more publicity than he wants for himself. We all, young and old, hope to make some sort of a name, but we want to make it in our own chosen way, and, if possible, by our own exertions. To be the hero of the '3 not out' in that heroic finish between Oxford and Cambridge (Under Ten), to be undisputed Fluff Weight Champion (four stone six) of the Lower School, even to be the only boy of his age who can do Long Division: any of these is worth much more than all your vicarious literary reputations. Lawrence hid himself in the Air Force under the name of Shaw to avoid being introduced for the rest of his life as 'Lawrence of Arabia'. I do not want C. R. Milne ever to wish that his names were Charles Robert.

The comparison between Lawrence of Arabia and Christopher Robin, which at first seems rather ridiculous, has real reverberations. Robert Graves once wrote of Lawrence, 'He both despised and loved the legend that surrounded him', and this was also true of Christopher Milne at different stages of his life. The great difference, of course, was that Lawrence's legend was based on his own achievements, Christopher Robin's on nothing he had done himself – and his mixed feelings would eventually transfer from the legend to his father, the author of it.

Milne had another reason to stop writing for children. A writer has to believe that his latest book is his best:

Can I go on writing these books, and persuade myself that each is better than the one before? I don't see how it is possible. Darwin, or somebody, compared the world of knowledge to a circle of light. The bigger the circumference of light, the bigger the surrounding border of darkness waiting to be lit up. A child's world of the imagination is not like that. As children we have explored it from end to end, and the map of it lies buried somewhere in our hearts, drawn in symbols whose meaning we have forgotten. A gleam from outside may light it up for us, so that for a moment it becomes clear again, and in that precious moment we can make a copy of it for others. But when the light has gone, to go on making fair copies of that copy – is it worth it?

For writing, let us confess it unashamed, is fun. There are those who will tell you that it is an inspiration, they sing but as the linnet sings; there are others, in revolt against such priggishness, who will tell you that it is simply a business like any other. Others, again, will assure you (heroically) that it is an agony, and they would sooner break stones – as well they might. But though there is something of inspiration in it, something of business, something, at times, of agony, yet, in the main, writing is just thrill; the thrill of exploring. The more difficult the country, the more untraversed by the writer, the greater (to me, anyhow) the thrill.

Well, I have had my thrill out of children's books, and know that I shall never recapture it. At least, not until I am a grandfather.

A. A. Milne never did know himself to be a grandfather. His only grandchild, Clare, was born, severely disabled, a few months after his death.

Milne called that essay 'The End of a Chapter', as he came to the end of the five years or so in which he had been involved in writing the four children's books for which he will always be remembered. There was another much longer chapter – indeed one should rather call it a book – that was also coming to an end. Just after *The House at Pooh Corner* was published his brother Ken became seriously ill. He had been ill with tuberculosis for years, but he had learned to live with it, to move around, to live a quiet but almost normal life. Now he had to take to his bed.

At first his brother was not really alarmed. Ken had been in bed before. There was no reason to suppose he would not recover from this setback. Ken was having the best medical advice and treatment his brother could procure for him. 'Don't be afraid of having another specialist if you want one,' Milne wrote. In his next letter he told Ken he had seen Christopher as Sir Andrew Aguecheek in *Twelfth Night*: 'It's a rotten part. For pages at a time he says nothing but "Ay, 'tis so" and, after an enormous wait, "And me too." But he did make an effort to keep the thing going, and other people say he was very good. I suppose my standards of acting are too high.' It was the first time, but it would not be the last, that Christopher disappointed his father. He went on:

The Fourth Wall is a great go in New York. But I get terrible set-backs to make up. A Scarborough school-master wrote to ask if they could do a scene from Pooh *without paying a fee. Daff wrote back certainly as long as it was a private performance etc, etc. Now he writes: 'I wrote to you last Sunday, and received a reply from 'Celia Brice'. I was not asking her but you. As you write (if you have written it) in this discourteous way, the dramatisation of that, or of any other scene in any of your works can go to blazes, and you with it. Yours faithfully.' So I have nothing to hope from Scarborough.*

Life was not always plain sailing, even for the rich and healthy. 'The Fiat broke down next to the Nurse Cavell statue and had to be towed home. I haven't heard yet when if ever I shall see it again.' Milne ended his letter. 'Get well, please. Ever your very very affectionate, Alan.' In the months to come, he would say that over and over again: 'Get well, please.'

Even at this difficult time, Ken's wife Maud organised a special pencil with his name on it for Christopher's Christmas present. Alan sent them not a cheque but a large bank note, hoping that would make it more likely that they would spend it on something nice but 'entirely unnecessary'. 'A happy Christmas to you with your family,' Alan wrote to Ken, not allowing himself to realise it would be the last time he could send such a greeting. 'I hope that you will all have a happier New Year.'

Daphne and Alan Milne went to Grindelwald for skiing in February 1929; Ken and Alan had been there together in 1907, soon after Alan had joined *Punch*. Ken was much in his mind. He recalled an enormous walk they had done together. He showed it to everyone on the map and 'nobody believes it'. His last visit to Switzerland had been in 1913 – when he and Daphne had become engaged. He thought of that time too:

> *Sixteen years ago, I just went down moderate slopes, fall-ing at the bottom and Daff didn't go down, collapsing at the top. But there appears to be a lot more in it than that. Everybody here is terribly keen and many of them terribly good. Some of the things they do are beautiful to watch, and I feel, as I feel about anything I can't do, that I would sooner do this one thing than everything which I can do. (Which isn't much.)*

He told Ken about a *Boy's Own Paper* lunch he had been to just before going to Switzerland:

> *The Editor in replying to Baldwin's toast told us of some of the questions boys ask him; and said that one boy – about 10 by his writing – asked for the price of an expedition to the North or South Pole, 'for one man and his dog'. I gave one great 'O-oh!' when I heard this, and unaccountably found a tear trickling down my nose.*

He knew Ken would understand why he was so moved. He was weeping for the boys that he and Ken had been. He was weeping for lost childhood and for all the expeditions and adventures that they had had together, the two boys and their dog, a long-ago mongrel called Brownie. He was also weeping, perhaps, for the fact that life, rewarding and comfortable as it was, had not given him the challenges that he had imagined as a child, that the only snow he knew was the snow of safe comfortable Switzerland, not of the North Pole.

Above all, Milne was weeping for the brother he was losing. Ken died on 21 May 1929, aged forty-nine. His most vivid link with his childhood had gone. Memory, that wellspring of his best writing for children, was now painful.

AFTERWORD

Alan Milne lived another twenty-eight years after the death of his brother Ken, and after his decision to stop writing about Christopher Robin. But neither he nor the boy himself could avoid the particular kind of fame the children's books had brought them. When Milne went to America in 1931, ostensibly to publicise his new adult novel, *Two People*, and to discuss plans for a new play, he found nearly all the questions in bookshops and at parties were about Christopher Robin and Winnie-the-Pooh. Two years later the American *Parents* magazine named Christopher Robin as one of the five most famous children in the world.

The thirties were a time when Alan and Daphne were increasingly leading separate lives. Daphne's enthusiasm for the Pooh books and all the celebrity associated with them was itself a cause of friction between husband and wife at a time when Milne sometimes wished he had never written them. Daphne was finding the quiet life Milne liked (golf, watching cricket, and crossword puzzles, when he wasn't writing) was not enough to satisfy her. There is plenty of evidence that both of them found some happiness with other people. Alan Milne would say: 'Don't miss any happiness that is going or you will find it gone.' He felt only children can experience unalloyed happiness. When we are adult, 'happiness is always tainted with the knowledge that one will have to pay for it.' There were important relationships, but the marriage survived.

Alan Milne's father died in 1932. All the links with his childhood were now severed. He had spent a great deal of his adult life looking forward to the next thing he was about to write, the next piece for *Punch*, the next play, the next book, full of optimism. It had always seemed that he was making his reputation. But now he had to accept that he had made it and it was not the one that he had wanted.

We do not need, in this version of Milne's story, to read much about the strains and stresses of the thirties, even the politics, the rise of fascism, with which Milne told an interviewer his mind was 'intolerably preoccupied'. There was the singular success of just one of his books, *Peace with Honour*, in 1934, his tract against war. At that point Milne was temporarily famous for something other than being the father of Christopher Robin, but the odds were stacked against his pacifist views. They came to be seen as 'appeasement' and Milne himself would admit that there were some things that had to be fought. Six years later, he would publish *War with Honour*. For the most part, there were sluggish sales of his adult books and bad reviews of his plays.

Just one play, *Toad of Toad Hall* (an adaptation of his favourite book) was enthusiastically received. It had been first suggested by Curtis Brown in 1921, but was not finally produced until 1929. It continued to be a Christmas treat for children for many years, until in the twenty-first century it was supplanted by Alan Bennett's *The Wind in the Willows*.

Milne came to hate the word 'whimsical' in his reviews and the constant references to the Pooh books. Even if he wrote something as straightforward as 'the cat sat on the mat', he said, he would be accused of being whimsical about cats, 'not a real cat, but just a little make-believe pussy, such as the author of *Winnie-the-Pooh* invents so charmingly for our delectation'.

When *Sarah Simple* was produced in 1940 in America, one critic would reflect that the man who had written such excellent plays as *Mr Pim Passes By*, *The Truth about Blayds* and *The Dover Road*, 'now writes with about as much maturity as Christopher Robin'. It was a hard time, of course, a time when theatre reviews seemed particularly irrelevant. But he now knew it would not be as a playwright that he would be remembered.

A. A. Milne was now richer than he would ever have believed possible. It seemed churlish to grumble. Pooh had already become an industry in the thirties. Vast sales of all four of the books, with translations all over the world, had stimulated the sales of 'hygienic plush toys', board games, calendars, jigsaw puzzles, writing paper and nursery china. There were endless spin-offs from the books: *Hums*, *Songs*, the *Christopher Robin Story Book*, the *Christopher Robin Reader*, the *Christopher Robin Verses* (with twelve colour plates) and so on. In America, the total sales of the four central books had already reached a million copies. Eeyore, Tigger, Piglet and the rest were on their way to becoming lodged permanently in what could be called the folk-memories of the English-speaking people, part of our common language and frame of reference.

The most important thing for Alan Milne in the 1930s was his relationship with his son. As Christopher himself put it in *The Enchanted Places*: 'My father, who had derived such happiness from his childhood, found in me the companion with whom he could return there.' Not long after Ken's death, the time had come for Olive Rand, to whom Christopher had been so devoted, to leave. At last she felt free to marry; Milne furnished her cottage, which she called Vespers, as a wedding present. At nine, Christopher was off to a boarding prep school, but in the holidays there would be no one to come between father and son, as there always had been when the boy's first love was his nanny.

For Milne, Christopher could be, as he grew up, what his brother Ken had been in their boyhood. After Ken's death, the letters to the invalid Ken in Somerset became letters to Christopher at school. In the holidays, at Cotchford, in London and in Dorset, they did things together more and more. For the next ten years the boy was his father's closest friend. It even seemed, at this early stage, that he might become a first-class cricketer. Milne wrote to an old friend: 'He is always the youngest boy in any form he is in and generally top. Forgive a proud parent; he is a duck.' Christopher had a passion for knowledge, for algebra, for learning the Greek alphabet. They shared ball games, crosswords, Euclid, morse.

In the summer of 1934, Milne described his son as he turned fourteen. 'Moon left his prep school in July, being then top of the school, leader of the choir, captain of cricket and in the football XI.' He had won a scholarship to Stowe, his father's choice. Milne was still happily unaware how much his son was coming to resent his celebrity. The boy did not blame his father at this stage, but 'Christopher Robin', as he himself put it, 'was beginning to be, what he was later to become, a sore place that looked as if it would never heal.'

In 1936, Milne reported to a friend that the boy 'is the most completely modest, unspoilt, enthusiastic happy darling in the world. In short, I adore him.' Christopher, who had described his father as 'buttoned up all through his life', did not of course read this letter until he came across it in my biography. It was at this point that boys in the next study at Stowe were playing the record of 'Vespers' over and over again on their wind-up gramophone and driving the 'happy darling' into despair. He was very vulnerable, but most of the time he could forget the books and the bear and get on with his work. He was an even better mathematician than his father, but his cricket, which might have helped him, did not fulfil his father's hopes; he got no further than the Third Eleven.

Four years running in the mid-thirties, father and son had holidays in rented houses on the Dorset coast with Ken's widow and three of his children, Christopher's cousins. Maud, aged fifty, organised the meals. The other five played and swam. Christopher recalled, 'For us, to whom our childhood had meant so much, the journey back is short, the coming and going easy.' Sometimes there were boats, sometimes tennis courts. Always there was the sea and crosswords and endless paper games.

More and more, Milne found himself looking back, not ahead. In 1938, at the height of the Munich crisis, this was understandable. He was writing his *Autobiography*, published under that title in America and as *It's Too Late Now* in Britain. In it, Milne devoted more than half to his own beginnings – child, schoolboy, undergraduate – and only a few pages to the four famous children's books, though he must have realised that that was the section that would most interest people. Of Christopher, he said little beyond the fact that they had intended to call their child Rosemary, but decided later that Billy would be more suitable. In the end, he was registered as Christopher Robin, 'names wasted on him who called himself Billy Moon as soon as he could talk, and has been Moon to his family and friends ever since. I mention this because it explains why the publicity attached to "Christopher Robin" never seemed to affect us personally, but rather to concern a character in a book.'

The boy had certainly shown no signs of any normal adolescent rebellion. What he had begun to show were the signs of nervous tension, of an increasing shyness, the outward expression, presumably, of a subconscious worry that he could never fulfil his father's deepest ambitions for him, that he could never be the sort of debonair young man readers expected that charming, competent child, Christopher Robin, to become – if, indeed, they imagined him growing up at all. The schoolboy Christopher Milne both trembled and stammered and remained anxious in all he did to please his father.

In 1939, in that last beautiful summer before war was declared, on holiday together on Dartmoor, father and son were still extremely close and would remain so throughout the war. This was in spite of the fact that for much of that time they were separated by many hundreds of miles. Christopher went up to Milne's old college, Trinity, Cambridge, in the autumn that year.

Milne found solace in practising his long-neglected talent for light verse in a sort of rhyming war diary that appeared in *Punch* in the first year of the war. When it was published in October 1940 as *Behind the Lines*, the book was dedicated:

To my affinity:
C. R. Milne: Mathematical scholar of Trinity:
And: By the time this appears:
With any luck Private in the Royal Engineers.

Christopher had failed his first medical through trembling with nervous excitement, but his father's intervention had given him another chance. The boy was keen to go and managed to pass a trade test and in July 1942 he was finally commissioned and sailed for the Middle East with a battalion of the Royal Engineers.

It was the war that would eventually allow him to make the necessary escape from his father, to be himself, to put his childhood finally behind him. Those five years, he would say, 'provided me with a foundation stone, strong and lasting, on which to build my adult life.'

Milne was writing letters to destinations all over the Middle East, North Africa and Italy. Christopher was in Lombardy when, on 7 October 1944, the dreaded telegram arrived in Cotchford. It was not that the boy was missing, but rather, and equally frightening, that he had suffered 'a penetrating shell wound in the right occipital region and was seriously ill.' In fact the head wound, it turned out, was not very serious. Milne wrote a letter to *The Times*, objecting to the way the War Office had alarmed them.

There was no further occasion for similar suffering. But there would be other suffering to come for which Milne was hardly prepared. There was a girl in Trieste who 'helped to loosen the bond that tied' the boy to his father.

Milne had often said he wanted his son to stand on his own two feet and make his own name for himself. But when Christopher at last started out on that path, his father found it extremely difficult.

It was the period after the war that caused the final rift. The young man, like so many returned soldiers, found it difficult to get work. He had gone back to Cambridge to finish his degree, had switched to English and finished with a mere Third:

> In pessimistic moments, when I was trudging London in search of an employer wanting to make use of such talents as I could offer, it seemed to me, almost, that my father had got to where he was by climbing upon my infant shoulders, that he had filched from me my good name and had left me with nothing but the empty fame of being his son.

Now it seems they had only one thing in common: 'If I wanted to escape from Christopher Robin, so, too, did he.'

The strength of the bond that there had been between father and son made the breaking of it all the more painful. Almost the last time they were in the same room was when Christopher married his cousin, Lesley de Sélincourt.

They had been introduced by their shared step-grandmother, sorry that they did not know each other. Lesley's father, Aubrey, had been estranged from Christopher's mother, Daphne, for many years. The marriage would not 'bury their parents' strife'. Christopher was joining Lesley in the opposing camp. Lesley had no time at all for *Winnie-the-Pooh*.

In 1951, Christopher and Lesley set up their own bookshop in Dartmouth in Devon. Their story together went on for nearly fifty years and enabled Christopher to say in the preface to his second memoir *The Path Through the Trees* that he had had a happy life. He never completely got over his dislike of being the real live Christopher Robin, but when he looked at the four famous books in his shop, he admitted finally he could not help being proud of his father. He was proud himself of the fact that he and his wife were self-supporting at the Harbour Bookshop. His share of his father's fortune went into a Trust for his disabled daughter, a Trust that continues after Clare's death in 2012, to support disabled people in south-west England.

A. A. Milne's last years were not happy, though he and Daphne lived amicably in their home on the edge of Ashdown Forest and he had come to terms at last with his claim to immortality, and his most famous creation,

Winnie-the-Pooh. He wrote to a young fan: 'There was a period when any reference to him was infuriating, but now such a "nice comfortable feeling" envelops him that I can almost regard him impersonally as the creation of one of my own favourite authors.'

It was an odd remark. Perhaps at last he was seeing that his four books deserved to be on the same special shelf as *The Wind in the Willows*.

In 1926, just after *Winnie-the-Pooh* was published, A. A. Milne had written: 'I suppose that every one of us hopes secretly for immortality; to leave, I mean, a name behind him which will live for ever in this world, whatever he may be doing himself in the next.' There is no doubt that he had achieved – though not in the way he had wished – that certain immortality.

A. A. Milne died after a long illness in 1956. Christopher Robin Milne died forty years later.

PICTURE ACKNOWLEDGEMENTS

All photographs are from the author's own collection with the exception of the following:

Page 1, *left* and page 5, *top*: Line illustrations copyright © E. H. Shepard. Reproduced with permission of Curtis Brown Group Ltd on behalf of The Shepard Trust

Page 2, *top*: © E. O. Hoppé / Corbis

Page 2, *bottom* and page 3, *top* and *bottom*: © Bettmann

Page 4, *top and bottom* and page 8, *bottom*: © Brian Sibley

Page 6: Text by A. A. Milne copyright © Trustees of the Pooh Properties, reproduced with the permission of Curtis Brown Group Ltd

Page 7, *bottom*: © The New York Public Library, Astor, Lennox and Tilden Foundations